THE ART OF
THE CAKE

THE ART OF THE CAKE

THE ULTIMATE STEP-BY-STEP GUIDE TO BAKING AND DECORATING PERFECTION

MICH TURNER MBE

OF LITTLE VENICE CAKE COMPANY

with photography by MALOU BURGER

UNIVERSE

DEDICATION
For Marvellous Marlow and Gorgeous George, with love

Publisher's note: This book includes some recipes containing raw eggs.
It is advisable to avoid serving these dishes to pregnant or nursing mothers
and those with compromised immune systems.

First published in the United States of America in 2011 by
UNIVERSE PUBLISHING
A Division of Rizzoli International Publications, Inc.
300 Park Avenue South
New York, NY 10010
www.rizzoliusa.com

Originally published in the United Kingdom as
Mich Turner's Cake Masterclass in 2011 by
Jacqui Small
An imprint of Aurum Books Ltd
7 Greenland Street
London NW1 0ND

PUBLISHER Jacqui Small
EDITORIAL MANAGER Kerenza Swift
EDITOR Alison Bolus
ART DIRECTOR Ashley Western
PRODUCTION Peter Colley

2011 2012 2013 2014 / 10 9 8 7 6 5 4 3 2 1

ISBN: 978-0-7893-2215-9

Library of Congress Control Number: 2010932890

Printed in Singapore

Contents

Welcome to my Master class. In this book I will give you the tools, techniques, and tips required to introduce you to the world of perfect cake making, baking, and decorating. Whether you are looking to learn a new skill as a complete novice, increase your repertoire as a keen decorator, or enhance your skills as a semi-professional, I hope this book will encourage, inspire, and tutor you effectively to create some amazing cakes.

We start with Essential Equipment, which identifies the specialist tools you will need, followed by Cake Baking, which contains many methods to guarantee perfect results. Try them out to find your favorites.

In Fillings and Frostings, I give you a number of recipes you can use to fill and frost your cakes, from a simple afternoon teatime cake to a luxury creation.

Careful Covering and Stacking will show you how to cover and stack your cakes flawlessly, pointing out many of the potential pitfalls to avoid to ensure you have the perfect cake all ready for additional decoration.

The Master Class section will show you in detail how to achieve many of the techniques I use in everyday cake decorating, from hand piping, painting, and molding to using cutters and ribbons.

Finally, the Cake Gallery is where the inspiration comes alive, as many of the techniques from the master class are put into practice.

My aim has been to provide you with a comprehensive manual of cake decorating. I am sure this could lead to several volumes.

Be inspired!

Paint palette for
mixing color

Color dusts

Paintbrushes

Assorted flower petal cutters

Tips in various sizes and shapes

Concentric round cutters

Smiley tool

Small ball tool

Large ball tool

Pokey tool

Shell / marking tool

Retractable pokey tool

Edible glitter

Assorted ribbons—grosgrain, double satin, and organza in plain and patterned versions

Flower plunger cutters

Essential Equipment

Daffodil cutter

Heart metal cutter

Ribbon insertion tools

Daffodil cutter

Tools of the Trade

A skilled craftsman requires professional tools to carry out their work, and baking and decorating cakes are no exception. Make sure you have a set of measuring cups at hand. Mixing bowls can be glass, plastic, or stainless steel, but ensure you have some in different sizes: large, roomy bowls for aerating, creaming, and whisking, and smaller bowls for melting chocolate and weighing ingredients.

Cake making equipment

Hand-held balloon whisks (a), hand-held mixers (b), and larger table-top mixers are all useful for mixing larger quantities or for more controlled precision work for cakes, fillings, and frostings.

I like to use good-quality, sturdy pans to bake my cakes (c, d), whether plain or more fancy. Pans will remain rigid and are a good heat conductor, so are perfect for tiered cakes. Silicone molds are also good for the interestingly shaped cakes they create. The molds, which are now widely available, are nonstick and versatile enough to be used safely in the oven, freezer, microwave, and dishwasher.

Wire racks (e) are essential for cooling large and small cakes, and for holding cakes to be covered in poured chocolate ganache. Finally, sifters and strainers in various sizes (f, g) are useful for many tasks, such as sifting flour or dusting a cake or countertop with confectioners' sugar or cocoa powder.

Lining a pan

All cake pans need to be lined to protect the outer surfaces of the cake during the baking time. The technique is similar for a round or square pan.

1 Cut 2 sheets of parchment paper, either round or square, just a little smaller than the base of the pan. Brush the inside of the pan with melted butter or canola oil and place one liner in the bottom. Fold a long sheet of parchment paper in half lengthways, then fold the long folded edge up by ½ inch. Use a sharp pair of scissors to snip diagonally at 1-inch intervals from the first folded edge to the second fold.

2 Place the collar inside the pan, pushing the diagonal cut edge to fit neatly. Brush over the cut edge with melted butter or oil. Trim the top edge of the collar so it protrudes no higher than 1 inch above the height of the pan.

3 Place the second nonstick baking paper liner in the base of the pan to cover the cut bottom edge of the paper collar. The pan is now ready to be used.

a Large silicone rolling pin
b Pizza wheel
c Palette knife
d Serrated knife
e Small sharp knife
f Spatula
g Small silicone rolling pin
h Wooden spoon
i Pastry brush
j Icing smoothers
k Nonslip turntable

Cake filling, covering, and decorating equipment

A large serrated knife can be used to split cakes, and a selection of palette knives is useful to spread buttercreams and cream cheese frostings.

Use concentric metal cutters (see p. 8) in three sizes for cutting out what you need for individual cakes: one for the cake, one for the base coat, and one for the top coat.

I like to use silicone rolling pins for rolling out marzipan, rolled fondant, and chocolate plastique. Silicone retains its temperature and gives the paste a smooth, even finish, unlike marble, which can chill the paste, or wood, which can impart a grainlike texture. Rolling pins come in various sizes: larger pins for rolling out sheets of marzipan and smaller pins for feathering chocolate plastique collars and petal paste for models or flowers.

Pizza wheels are great for cutting pastes. Being a rotary cutter, a pizza wheel will not snag or pull the pastes.

Molded plastic icing smoothers are essential for a flawless finish, to achieve the smoothest coverings of marzipan, rolled fondant, and chocolate plastique. Invest in one molded-edged smoother for the tops of cakes and two straight-edged smoothers for the sides or for working on individual cakes.

Set cakes on a nonslip turntable for ease of decorating. An 8-inch size turntable is good for most individual cakes and single tiers, and a 14-inch lower turntable is perfect for working on stacked and tiered cakes.

Your professional kit should also include: a selection of stainless-steel piping tips, nonstick piping bags in different sizes, various paintbrushes, color dusts, color pastes, metallic lusters, cocoa butter, dipping alcohol, edible varnish, cutters, and modeling tools, including a ball tool. In addition, you will need three pairs of scissors: small precision scissors for ribbon, larger, general-purpose scissors for templates, and a heavy-duty pair for doweling rods. You will also need a pokey tool, fine-liner pen, and non-toxic pencil for transferring the template designs.

There are so many pretty, stylish cake stands and plates available in different sizes and shapes. I collect them whenever I see them—glass, fine porcelain, chunky china, hand painted, laser cut—you can never have too many to serve so many beautiful, fun, or stylish cakes.

PT. FL. OZ. ML
2 40
35
1000
30 900
800
25 700
600
20
15 500
400
10 300

SUGAR FLOUR
OZ. 32 20 OZ.
28 16
24
20 12
16
12 8
8 4
4

Cake Baking

There are several methods of cake making, resulting in different style cakes. In this chapter I will show and explain the basic methods, which include creaming, melting, straight mixing, and whisking, plus provide you with lots of delicious recipes. Some cakes have a delicious filling or frosting and are perfect for serving for afternoon tea, whereas others are more suited to being used as a base for covering and decorating. There are also those that are versatile enough to be considered for either. I will identify these where they are included in this chapter. As a rule of thumb, all ingredients should be at room temperature unless otherwise stated. I like to use unrefined sugars, organic flours, organic free-range eggs, 70% cocoa solids bittersweet chocolate, and fresh fruits for zesting.

Creaming

Cakes made by the creaming method rely on precise measurements, all the ingredients being at room temperature, and the batter being beaten well at each stage. They also need to have air incorporated at each of the beating stages to result in a well-risen cake, with even texture and a clean bite. The cake should not be dense or crumbly.

Beat the butter and sugar together until really light and fluffy. This should be done with an electric mixer and will take 10 minutes. If you do not have an electric mixer, you will have to use a wooden spoon and beat for a long time!

The eggs should be beaten together before being added a little at a time, with the mixer still beating, to prevent the batter from curdling (separating). If the batter does separate, simply add a spoonful of flour and continue beating in the egg. It will not ruin the cake, but the texture will be a little more dense.

Sift the flour in and fold it into the batter carefully with a metal spoon, to avoid breaking down the air bubbles that were created during the beating stages.

Stir in any final ingredients; transfer the batter to the pan carefully, to preserve as much air as possible.

Melting

Cakes made by the melting method are the most reliable and so are perfect for beginners. They rely on the addition of a strong leavener (baking soda), rather than the inclusion of air, to leaven the cake.

Melt the sugar and butter or oil together; combine this liquid with the eggs. Stir the dry ingredients into the batter before transferring it to the pan. Baking soda has a distinctive taste, so spices such as ginger, cinnamon, and nutmeg are often added to these cakes to mask the flavor. These cakes tend to be very moist, but are more dense in texture than other cakes.

Straight mixing

For straight mixing cakes, the ingredients must be at room temperature and accurately measured. The method is as simple as it sounds: You put all the ingredients into a bowl and beat them together with an electric mixer (or a wooden spoon, if you don't have a mixer) until they are well combined. In addition to using self-rising flour, you will need to add another leavener (in this case baking powder). Baking powder is a gentler leavener than baking soda, because although it does contain some baking soda, it is blended with cream of tartar, which counterbalances the harsh flavor. These cakes will have a similar, but more dense, texture to the creamed cakes.

TIP It is important to use fresh self-rising flour and baking power, as their potency does fade over time.

Whisking

Whisked cakes have very little, if any, fat in them, relying instead on air being incorporated when the eggs and sugar are whisked together. These cakes are incredibly light and airy, making them a good choice following a heavy meal, but must be eaten on the day they are made as they will dry out quickly, having no butter or oil to keep them moist.

Whisked cakes will generally be accompanied by a cream- or butter-based filling, frosting, or topping to introduce a fat content to keep them moist and balance the taste and texture.

Again, all ingredients should be at room temperature. Whisk the eggs and sugar until they are really pale and thick, which can take 10 minutes even with an electric mixer. Stir in all the other ingredients carefully to avoid breaking down the air bubbles.

Cherry and Almond Cake

Creaming • Cherries and almonds go together beautifully in this light yet moist cake. Although the cake is delicious on its own, I've added a sweet crunchy topping of some Demerara sugar and sliced almonds, which makes it that extra bit special! This cake keeps well and can be used as the base for a decorated celebration cake if it is baked without the crunchy topping. The photographs highlight the key stages involved in the creaming method. Do not be tempted to rush any of these stages, and ensure all the ingredients are at room temperature.

¾ cup plus 3 tbsp. unsalted butter, plus extra for greasing

heaping 1¼ cups unrefined superfine sugar

4 extra-large eggs, lightly beaten

1¾ cups all-purpose flour

½ tsp. baking powder

1¼ cups ground almonds

1 cup naturally colored candied cherries, quartered

1 tsp. almond extract

1 tbsp. milk

2 tbsp. Demerara sugar

2 tbsp. sliced blanched almonds

bake: convection 325°F
conventional 350°F

1 Preheat the oven. Put the butter and sugar in a bowl.

2 Start beating them together.

3 Continue beating until the batter is light, pale, and fluffy.

4 Gradually beat in the eggs, a little at a time.

5 Sift the flour and baking powder into the bowl.

6 Carefully fold into the creamed batter, using a metal spoon.

7 Add the ground almonds.

8 Add the candied cherries, almond extract, and milk.

9 Carefully fold into the batter.

10 Spoon the cake batter into a greased and lined 8-inch cake pan.

11 Level off the top with the back of a spoon.

12 Sprinkle with the Demerara sugar and sliced almonds.

13 This will form the crunchy topping when the cake is cooked.

14 Bake the cake in the center of the oven 1 hour; cover with foil and continue cooking 15 to 20 minutes more, or until the cake has shrunk away from the sides of the pan, the center is springy to touch, and a skewer inserted into the middle of the cake comes out clean. Leave the cake to cool in the pan 15 minutes before turning it out onto a wire rack to cool completely.

*TO STORE Store in an airtight container or wrapped in waxed paper or foil up to 1 week. Alternatively, wrap the cake in a double layer of waxed paper and foil and place in the freezer up to 1 month.

Madagascan Berry Vanilla Cake

Creaming • For a truly authentic flavor, it is imperative to use seeds from vanilla beans to make this cake. The addition of Greek-style yogurt in the batter gives the cake a lovely texture, and the cake is finished off with a creamy berry topping.

For the cake:

1 cup unsalted butter, plus extra
    for greasing

heaping 1¼ cups unrefined
    superfine sugar

seeds from 1 vanilla bean

5 extra-large eggs, lightly beaten

⅔ cup all-purpose flour

2 cups self-rising flour

heaping ⅓ cup full-fat Greek-style
    yogurt

3 tbsp. milk

heaping ¾ cup raspberries

⅔ cup blueberries

For the topping:

1 cup crème fraîche

heaping ⅓ cup raspberries

⅓ cup blueberries

bake: convection 325˚F
    conventional 350˚F

1 Preheat the oven. Grease and line a deep 8-inch cake pan with parchment paper or use a nonstick cake pan. Ensure all the ingredients are at room temperature. Beat the butter, sugar, and vanilla seeds together until they are light and fluffy (a).

2 Add the eggs a little at a time, beating well after each addition. If the batter starts to curdle, stir in 1 tablespoon of one of the flours. Beat in the yogurt. Sift the flours together and fold into the batter, followed by the milk. Spoon half the batter into the base of the prepared cake pan and stir the raspberries and blueberries into the remainder (b). Spoon this batter on top of the bottom layer and bake in the oven 1 hour 20 minutes.

3 Remove the cake from the oven and let cool a little on a wire rack; turn out and let cool completely. To serve, spoon the crème fraîche onto the top of the cake and dress with the raspberries and blueberries (c).

Note that this cake can settle and sink slightly overnight. It can therefore be a good idea to dowel tiers made using this recipe as close to the time of stacking or blocking as possible (see pp. 82–3), to ensure the cake is stable.

*TO STORE With no filling or topping, this cake will keep 7 days wrapped in waxed paper or covered with marzipan and icing or chocolate. Alternatively, wrap the cake in a double layer of waxed paper and aluminum foil and place in the freezer up to 1 month. This recipe is perfect to use as a base for a decorated celebration cake. Once the cake is filled and covered, it must be refrigerated and eaten on the day.

Chocolate Truffle Torte

Creaming • This cake, which is rich but not too sweet, is made with melted chocolate, so the texture is similar to that of a chocolate brownie. As there is comparatively very little flour, the recipe relies on the chocolate and eggs to support the finished cake. It can be covered with marzipan and icing, then decorated, or covered in chocolate ganache and served with fresh berries as a dessert. For a deep cake, you should split the batter between two 3-inch-deep cake pans (so the cake cooks evenly while retaining a good height), then sandwich together with buttercream. For a single-depth cake, just one of the cakes is used. Individual small cakes can be stamped out of a single-depth cake (see pp. 66 and 69).

a

1 Preheat the oven. Grease and line 2 deep cake pans of the correct size with parchment paper or use nonstick cake pans. Ensure all the ingredients are at room temperature. Melt the chocolate in a microwave or in a bowl over simmering water; let cool.

2 Beat the butter and sugar together until light and fluffy. Beat in the eggs a little at a time, beating well between each addition. Pour the chocolate in slowly (a), beating all the time. Stir in the vanilla extract; fold in the flour.

3 Spoon the batter evenly into the 2 prepared cake pans and bake for the time stated. The cakes should be well risen, with a crust, but will still wobble when shaken gently. Remove from the oven and let cool before turning out. The crust will sink back onto the cake—this is normal.

4 If decorating this cake, sandwich the 2 halves together with buttercream. For added luxury, slice each half horizontally and sandwich again.

*TO STORE This cake will keep up to 10 days once covered and decorated or wrapped in waxed paper and kept in an airtight container. Although it can be refrigerated if prepared in advance with fresh fruit, allow time for it to come up to room temperature to ensure the melted chocolate in the recipe adds to the truffle texture. It is suitable for freezing. Defrost overnight.

TIP Be careful not to overbake this cake, as it can become dry and crumbly.

FOR THE CAKE (round/square)	6-inch	8-inch/6-inch	10-inch/8-inch	12-inch/10-inch
bittersweet chocolate (70% cocoa solids) broken into pieces and melted	7 oz.	14 oz.	1 lb. 5 oz.	1 lb. 12 oz.
unsalted butter, plus extra for greasing	1 cup	2 cups	3 cups	4 cups
light brown sugar, lightly packed	scant 2 cups	3¾ cups	5⅔ cups	7½ cups
large eggs, lightly beaten	5	10	15	20
vanilla extract	1½ tsp.	1 tbsp.	1½ tbsp.	2 tbsp.
all-purpose flour, sifted	heaping 1 cup	2¼ cups	scant 3½ cups	scant 4½ cups
bake: convection 275°F conventional 325°F	45 minutes	1 hour	1 hour 20 minutes	1 hour 40 minutes

Chocolate and Cherry Cake

Creaming • This is the ultimate indulgent chocolate cake. French candied cherries are soaked in vintage port overnight, which gives this cake a wonderful richness and delicious flavor. Serve for dessert or a special afternoon tea, covered in smooth poured dark chocolate ganache.

a

For the cake:

1 cup unsalted butter, plus extra
    for greasing
9 oz. dark chocolate (70% cocoa solids)
scant 2 cups light brown sugar,
    lightly packed
5 large eggs
1 tsp. vanilla extract
½ cup whole French candied cherries,
    soaked overnight in ⅓ cup vintage port
heaping 1 cup all-purpose flour

For the topping:

½ recipe chocolate ganache buttercream
    (see p. 53), at room temperature
1 recipe chocolate ganache (see p. 50)
8 oz. fresh cherries

bake: convection 275°F
conventional 325°F

1 Preheat the oven. Grease and line a deep 8-inch round cake pan with parchment paper or use a nonstick cake pan. Ensure all the ingredients are at room temperature.

2 Melt the chocolate in a bowl over a pan of simmering water or in a microwave. Let cool.

3 Beat the butter and sugar together in a mixing bowl until light and fluffy. Add the eggs, one at a time, until they are all incorporated. Pour in the melted chocolate, beating all the time; stir in the vanilla extract (a). Finally, add the cherries with any remaining port. Sift the flour into the batter and fold in gently.

4 Spoon the batter into the prepared pan and bake 55 to 60 minutes. Let cool in the pan. Turn out onto a wire rack.

5 Following the instructions on p. 51 for pouring ganache, cover the top and sides with a thin coat of buttercream and chill in the refrigerator 15 minutes. When the cake is covered in ganache, use a palette knife to make waves on the top and to smooth the sides.

6 Let the ganache set 10 minutes before using a small knife to lever the cake from the rack and trim the base edge. Meanwhile, gather up the remaining ganache from under the wire rack and put it in a bowl. Once it has cooled a little and thickened, spoon it into a piping bag fitted with a star tip, ready to pipe.

7 Place the cake on a decorative stand. Pipe scrolls around the top edge of the cake in an alternating pattern, as shown, pulling each scroll to a tail before starting the next.

8 For the shells around the base, pipe a uniform trail with the ganache. Dress the cake with the fresh cherries.

TIP If the ganache firms up and becomes too stiff to pipe, remove and gently reheat and let cool again until it reaches the desired consistency.

*TO STORE Store this cake at room temperature and eat within 2 days. Alternatively, wrap the cake in a double layer of waxed paper and foil and place in the freezer up to 1 month.

Luscious Lemon Cake

Creaming • This has to be the supreme lemon cake. It is deliciously moist, fresh, and so lemony it never fails to impress. Serve it with a simple lemon curd buttercream or use it as a base covered with marzipan, rolled fondant, or chocolate plastique for a special celebration cake. Be sure to weigh the ingredients accurately, have them at room temperature, and ensure each stage is well creamed or beaten before moving on to the next step.

a

1 Grease and line the cake pan with parchment paper or use a nonstick cake pan. Ensure all the ingredients are at room temperature. Place the butter and sugar in a clean bowl and beat with an electric mixer until light and fluffy. Add the rest of the ingredients and mix to a fairly runny cake batter.

2 Transfer the batter into the prepared pan and bake for the relevant time, or until a skewer inserted into the middle of the cake comes out clean.

3 As soon as you have put the cake into the oven, combine the lemon juice and sugar for the syrup glaze in a bowl and leave until the sugar has completely dissolved.

4 Remove the cake from the oven and use a skewer to spike holes all over the cake, ensuring you reach all the way to the bottom. Pour the syrup over the cake and leave until the cake has absorbed it and is cool. Turn out onto a wire rack, cut into 3 layers and fill with lemon curd buttercream (see p. 52). Dust the top with confectioners' sugar.

Note that this cake can settle and sink slightly overnight. It can therefore be a good idea to dowel tiers made using this recipe as close to the time of stacking or blocking as possible, to ensure the cake is stable.

FOR THE CAKE	6-inch round	8-inch round/ 6-inch square	10-inch round/ 8-inch square	12-inch round/ 10-inch square
unsalted butter, plus extra for greasing	2/3 cup plus 1 tbsp.	1 1/3 cups	2 cups plus 2 tbsp.	2 3/4 cups plus 1 tbsp.
unrefined superfine sugar	scant 1 cup	scant 2 cups	scant 3 cups	3 3/4 cups
self-rising flour	scant 1 1/2 cups	2 3/4 cups	4 1/4 cups	heaping 5 1/2 cups
baking powder	1 tsp.	2 tsp.	1 tbsp.	4 tsp.
large eggs, lightly beaten	3	6	9	12
finely grated lemon zest	2 lemons	4 lemons	6 lemons	8 lemons
milk	5 tbsp.	scant 2/3 cup	scant 1 cup	1 1/4 cups
vanilla extract	1 tsp.	2 tsp.	1 tbsp.	4 tsp.
FOR THE SYRUP GLAZE				
lemon juice	2 lemons	4 lemons	6 lemons	8 lemons
granulated white sugar	1/3 cup	2/3 cup	1 cup	1 1/3 cups
bake: convection 325°F conventional 350°F	55 minutes	1 hour 10 minutes	1 1/2 hours	1 3/4 hours

Polly's Sticky Ginger Cake

Melting • There is nothing quite like the smell, let alone the taste, of a ginger cake. Warm, rich, and spicy, it is the ideal cake for a winter's afternoon tea by the fire. Because this cake is made by the melting method, you need to start off with some of the ingredients in a saucepan, but once they are melted you can pour them into a mixing bowl and stir in the remaining ingredients, just as you would for a cake made by the creaming method. The resulting texture will be moist and sticky, as every good ginger cake should be.

½ cup unsalted butter, plus extra for greasing

1⅔ cups dark muscovado sugar, lightly packed

2 eggs

scant ½ cup milk

2¾ cups all-purpose flour

1 tbsp. ground ginger

1 tsp. baking soda

½ cup finely chopped candied ginger

3 tbsp. corn syrup

bake: convection 325°F
conventional 350°F

a

b

c

1 Preheat the oven. Grease and line a deep 9 x 5-inch loaf pan with parchment paper or use a nonstick loaf pan. Ensure all the ingredients are at room temperature.

2 Put the butter and sugar in a large saucepan and melt over a low heat. Remove from the heat, pour into a mixing bowl, and stir well (a).

3 Add the eggs and milk and beat well (b). Sift the flour, ground ginger, and baking soda into the bowl (c).

4 Add the ginger and syrup and stir well to combine, breaking up any lumps of flour (d).

5 Pour the batter into the prepared pan and bake 1 hour or until a skewer inserted into the middle of the cake comes out clean. Leave the cake to cool in the loaf pan 5 minutes; turn out. Peel off the lining paper and let cool on a wire rack.

*TO STORE Store in an airtight container or wrapped in waxed paper or foil up to 1 week. Alternatively, wrap in waxed paper and foil and freeze up to 1 month.

TIP Baking soda reacts once it makes contact with liquid, so put the cake in the oven as soon as it is mixed.

d

Rich Fruit Celebration Cake

Melting • This fruit cake is tried and tested as being the best ever! This recipe revolutionizes other rich fruit cake recipes as it is made, rather unusually, by melting the butter and sugar together first, then stirring in all the delicious plump fruits that have been steeping in brandy for hours. This ensures the cake is really moist and fruity and bakes to give a dense, even result, while at the same time remaining flat on the top, which makes it perfect for using as a base for decorating. It is delicious on its own or can be covered in the traditional combination of marzipan and icing.

a

1 Grease and line a deep cake pan with parchment paper or use a nonstick cake pan. Wash the fruits and drain through a sieve. Pour into a bowl, and pour the brandy over the mixture. Leave to steep up to 6 hours.

2 Preheat the oven. Ensure all the ingredients are at room temperature. Melt the butter and sugar together in a saucepan, stirring until well mixed; pour into a mixing bowl. Add the molasses and mix well; add the eggs and mix again. Sift in the flour, baking powder, and spices and fold in well. Stir in the steeped fruit and remaining liquid, the candied ginger, and vanilla extract (a).

3 Spoon the batter into the prepared pan and bake until a skewer inserted into the middle of the cake comes out clean. Leave the cake to cool in the pan and turn out when cold.

*TO STORE Wrap in a double layer of waxed paper and a layer of foil. Store at room temperature to mature up to 6 weeks prior to the event. Once covered in marzipan and icing, this cake will keep 6 months longer at room temperature. Alternatively, store in the freezer wrapped in a double layer of waxed paper and double layer of foil pretty much indefinitely.

FOR THE CAKE	6-inch round/ square	8-inch round/ square	10-inch round/ square	12-inch round/ square
unsalted butter, plus extra for greasing	½ cup	1 cup	1½ cups	2 cups
naturally colored candied cherries, halved	¾ cup	1½ cups	2¼ cups	3 cups
golden raisins	1¼ cups	2½ cups	heaping 3¾ cups	heaping 5 cups
raisins	1¾ cups	scant 3⅔ cups	scant 5½ cups	7¼ cups
currants	heaping 1¾ cups	3⅔ cups	5½ cups	7⅓ cups
brandy	scant ½ cup	scant 1 cup	scant 1½ cups	scant 2 cups
dark muscovado sugar	⅔ cup	scant 1½ cups	2 cups	2¾ cups
molasses	1½ tsp.	1 tbsp.	1½ tbsp.	2 tbsp.
eggs, lightly beaten	3 large	5 extra-large	5 extra-large + 3 large	10 extra-large
all-purpose flour	1 cup	scant 2 cups	2¾ cups	heaping 3¾ cups
baking powder	¼ tsp.	½ tsp.	¾ tsp.	1 tsp.
ground cinnamon	¼ tsp.	½ tsp.	¾ tsp.	1 tsp.
ground ginger	¼ tsp.	½ tsp.	¾ tsp.	1 tsp.
ground nutmeg	¼ tsp.	½ tsp.	¾ tsp.	1 tsp.
ground cloves	⅛ tsp.	¼ tsp.	⅜ tsp.	½ tsp.
pumpkin pie spice	¼ tsp.	½ tsp.	¾ tsp.	1 tsp.
candied ginger, chopped	2 tbsp.	scant ¼ cup	¼ cup	⅓ cup
vanilla extract	¼ tsp.	½ tsp.	¾ tsp.	1 tsp.
bake: convection 250°F conventional 275°F	2 hours	2½ hours	3 hours	3½ hours

3/4 cup plus 1 tbsp. unsalted butter,
    cut into pieces, plus extra for greasing
1 1/3 cups Medjool dates, pitted
scant 1/2 cup golden raisins
1 2/3 cups light brown sugar, lightly packed
2 eggs, lightly beaten
2 tbsp chopped preserved stem ginger
grated zest of 2 lemons
1 tsp. vanilla extract
9 oz. tart cooking apples, peeled and
    cored, then grated or chopped
scant 1 2/3 cups all-purpose flour
1/2 tsp. baking powder

bake: convection 300°F
conventional 325°F

Queen Elizabeth Date Cake

Melting • Moist and tasty, this nutritious cake is sustaining and simple to make, and it turns out well every time. It can be covered with marzipan and rolled fondant and decorated for an impressive centerpiece, or simply enjoyed on its own served with English breakfast tea or some freshly brewed coffee.

1 Preheat the oven. Grease and line a deep 6-inch round cake pan or deep 9 x 5-inch loaf pan with parchment paper, or use a nonstick pan. Ensure all the ingredients are at room temperature.

2 Place the dates and golden raisins in a bowl and cover with boiling water. Melt the butter and light brown sugar together in a saucepan and let cool slightly. Beat the eggs, ginger, lemon zest, and vanilla extract into the butter and sugar. Drain the fruit and chop the dates finely. Add to the saucepan with the apples and mix well. Sift in the flour and baking powder and fold in well.

3 Spoon the batter into the pan and bake in the oven about 1 1/4 hours until well risen and a skewer inserted into the middle of the cake comes out clean. Let cool in the pan.

*TO STORE This cake lasts 1 week if wrapped in waxed paper and foil and stored in an airtight container. Alternatively, wrap the cake in a double layer of waxed paper and foil and place in the freezer up to 1 month. It is delicious if kept in the refrigerator and served cold.

Moist Carrot Cake

Melting • This carrot cake recipe is universally adored. It is made with oil rather than butter, which puts it into the melted category of cakes, so results are pretty much guaranteed! It is a lighter alternative to a rich fruit cake but still very fruity, zesty, and spicy. It is baked with walnuts, rum-soaked golden raisins, and coconut. Once the cake is baked, it is spiked with a fresh citrus syrup, which helps to keep the cake moist. This cake is baked without dairy products, so is suitable for people with a dairy intolerance. It isn't necessary to add a filling or topping—but for a special celebration, fill the cake with a layer of orange buttercream (see p. 52) prior to covering with marzipan, icing, and decorating the cake. Alternatively, for a teatime treat, top the cake with some orange cream cheese frosting (see p. 56) and decorate with some chopped walnuts.

FOR THE CAKE (round/square)	6-inch	8-inch/6-inch	10-inch/8-inch	12-inch/10-inch
sunflower/canola oil, plus extra for greasing	scant $2/3$ cup	$1\frac{1}{4}$ cups	scant 2 cups	scant $2\frac{1}{2}$ cups
dark rum	1 tbsp. plus 2 tsp.	3 tbsp. plus 1 tsp.	5 tbsp.	6 tbsp. plus 2 tsp.
golden raisins	heaping $3/4$ cup	scant $1\frac{2}{3}$ cups	scant $2\frac{1}{2}$ cups	$3\frac{1}{4}$ cups
all-purpose flour	scant $1\frac{1}{2}$ cups	$2\frac{3}{4}$ cups	$4\frac{1}{4}$ cups	6 cups
ground cinnamon	2 tsp.	4 tsp.	2 tbsp.	2 tbsp. plus 2 tsp.
ground nutmeg	1 tsp.	2 tsp.	1 tbsp.	4 tsp.
baking soda	1 tsp.	2 tsp.	1 tbsp.	4 tsp.
unrefined superfine sugar	heaping $1/3$ cup	heaping $3/4$ cup	heaping $1\frac{1}{4}$ cups	$1\frac{2}{3}$ cups
light brown sugar, lightly packed	heaping $1/3$ cup	heaping $3/4$ cup	heaping $1\frac{1}{4}$ cups	$1\frac{2}{3}$ cups
large eggs	2	4	6	8
grated lemon zest	1	2	3	4
grated orange zest	1	2	3	4
grated carrots	1 cup	2 cups	3 cups	4 cups
shredded sweetened coconut	$1/2$ cup	1 cup	$1\frac{1}{2}$ cups	2 cups
walnuts, chopped	$1/3$ cup	$2/3$ cup	1 cup	$1\frac{1}{3}$ cups
vanilla extract	1 tsp.	2 tsp.	1 tbsp.	4 tsp.
candied ginger, chopped (optional)	2 tsp.	1 tbsp.	$1\frac{1}{2}$ tbsp.	2 tbsp.
FOR THE CITRUS SYRUP				
lemon(s), juiced	1	2	2	3
orange(s), juiced	1	1	2	2
light brown sugar	scant $1/3$ cup	$2/3$ cup	heaping $3/4$ cup	heaping $1\frac{1}{4}$ cups
bake: convection 260°F conventional 300°F	$1\frac{1}{2}$ hours	2 hours	$2\frac{1}{2}$ hours	3 hours

1 Grease and line a deep cake pan of the correct size with parchment paper or use a nonstick cake pan. Ensure all the ingredients are at room temperature (a). Pour the rum over the golden raisins and let infuse 1 hour.

2 Preheat the oven. Sift the flour together with the spices and the baking soda. Beat together the sugars, sunflower oil, and eggs until smooth. Stir the spiced flour into the smooth batter; add the remaining ingredients (including the candied ginger, if using) and stir well.

3 Spoon the batter into the prepared pan and bake for the time stated or until a skewer inserted into the middle of the cake comes out clean.

4 Make the syrup while the cake is baking. Strain the juices into a pitcher, add the sugar, and stir well. Continue to stir at intervals while the cake is in the oven. As soon as the cake is out of the oven, pierce it with a skewer several times (b) and carefully spoon or pour the citrus syrup over the top. Let cool before removing the cake from the pan.

*TO STORE This cake keeps fresh up to 2 weeks if covered and decorated with icing or wrapped in waxed paper and kept in an airtight container. Alternatively, wrap the cake in a double layer of waxed paper and foil and place in the freezer up to 1 month. Let defrost overnight.

Mocha Coffee Cake

Straight mixing • Coffee and chocolate have a strong affinity. Surely there is nothing more comforting than a hunk of chocolate cake with a freshly brewed mug of coffee? Here I have combined the two, using the simplest straight mixing method to make the chocolate cake, then adding a velvety smooth coffee frosting.

1 Preheat the oven. Grease and line two 8-inch round cake pans with parchment paper, or use nonstick cake pans. Ensure all the ingredients are at room temperature. Put all the cake ingredients into a large clean bowl (a) and whisk with a handheld electric mixer 8 to 10 minutes, until light and airy (b).

2 Divide the batter between the prepared pans (c) and bake 20 to 25 minutes, until the cake has shrunk away from the sides of the pan and is springy to the touch, and a skewer inserted into the middle of the cake comes out clean. Let cool in the pans a few minutes before turning out onto a wire rack to cool completely.

3 Spread one cake with half of the coffee frosting and place the other cake on top. Spread the remaining frosting over the top cake and decorate with chocolate curls.

Variations
Variations can be made by replacing the cocoa with more flour, then adding:

- the seeds from 2 vanilla beans for a *vanilla cake*
- 2 tbsp. ground cinnamon for a *spiced cake*
- the grated zest of 1 orange and 1 lemon for a *citrus cake*

For an alternative frosting, use vanilla cream cheese frosting (see p. 56).

*TO STORE Once the frosting is on the cake, eat the same day.

For the cake:
3/4 cup plus 1 tbsp. unsalted butter, plus extra for greasing
2/3 cup unsweetened cocoa powder
heaping 1 cup self-rising flour
heaping 1 cup unrefined superfine sugar
4 eggs, lightly beaten
2 tbsp. milk

For the filling and topping:
1 recipe coffee cream cheese frosting (see p. 56)
chocolate curls made using 2 oz. bittersweet chocolate (see p. 60)

bake: convection 325°F
conventional 350°F

Lemon and Poppy Seed Cake

Straight mixing • This cake, with its combination of a zesty fresh lemon sponge and crunchy poppy seeds, is a winner. I have chosen to bake this cake in a classic kugelhopf pan, which is a great way to add visual interest to a plainer cake. The most appropriate topping for this cake is a lemon glacé icing—adding flavor, sweetness, and moisture without detracting from the sharp flavor and interesting texture of the cake itself.

For the cake:

³/₄ cup plus 1 tbsp. unsalted butter,
    plus extra for greasing

1³/₄ cups self-rising flour, plus extra for
    dusting

heaping 1 cup unrefined superfine sugar

4 extra-large eggs

2 tbsp. milk

grated zest of 2 lemons

2 tbsp. poppy seeds

For the topping:

1 recipe lemon glacé icing (see p. 58)
fresh edible flowers

bake: convection 325°F
conventional 350°F

1 Preheat the oven. Grease and flour the base and sides of a 6-inch round kugelhopf pan. Ensure all the ingredients are at room temperature. Put all the ingredients into a large bowl and beat with an electric mixer 8 to 10 minutes. Pour the batter into the prepared pan.

2 Bake 25 to 35 minutes until the cake has shrunk away from the sides of the pan and is springy to the touch. Let cool in the pan a few minutes before turning out onto a wire rack to cool completely.

3 Cover with lemon glacé icing and decorate with fresh edible flowers.

*TO STORE Store up to 5 days in an airtight container. Alternatively, wrap the cake in a double layer of waxed paper and foil and place in the freezer up to 1 month.

Lime and Coconut Butterfly Buns

Straight mixing • These deliciously fresh cakes combine the zest of fresh limes with creamed coconut. The recipe given here will make 24 butterfly cakes or one 8-inch cake. A large cake works well covered with marzipan and rolled fondant, and makes a great and unusual alternative for a birthday or christening cake.

For the cakes:
³/₄ cup plus 1 tbsp. unsalted butter
heaping 1 cup unrefined superfine sugar
scant 1²/₃ cups self-rising flour
4 eggs, lightly beaten
2 tbsp. milk
3¹/₂ oz. creamed coconut, grated

For the lime syrup:
scant ¹/₃ cup unrefined superfine sugar
grated zest and juice of 1 lime

For the topping:
1 recipe lime frosting (see p. 57)
scant 1 cup toasted shredded coconut or
    coconut flakes

bake: convection 325°F
conventional 375°F

1 Preheat the oven. Line 2 cupcake tins with paper liners or place 24 silicone cupcake liners on a baking sheet. Ensure all the ingredients are at room temperature. Put all the cake ingredients into a large bowl (a) and whisk together until you have a smooth batter.

2 Spoon the batter into the liners, filling to two-thirds full. Bake in the oven 15 to 20 minutes until risen and light golden and the cakes spring back when pressed.

3 Meanwhile, place all the syrup ingredients and 3 tablespoons water in a saucepan and heat gently until dissolved. Brush each cake with the syrup as it comes out of the oven; let cool on a wire rack.

4 Cut an inverted cone from the top of each cake by inserting a small sharp knife at an angle and cutting all the way round (b). Remove this cone, cut in half vertically (to make "wings"), and put to one side.

5 Fit a piping bag with a large star tip and fill with the lime frosting; pipe it into the top of each cake until it is full.

6 Position the wings in the frosting (c). Sprinkle with toasted shredded coconut or coconut flakes.

*TO STORE Store in an airtight container and eat within 2 days. Not suitable for freezing.

Cinnamon and White Chocolate Cupcakes

Straight mixing • These cupcakes are deliciously moist, and the white chocolate buttercream makes them a decadent inclusion at any festive party. You could make even smaller, bite-size cupcakes and serve them at a chic canapé party, or present them in small boxes tied with ribbon.

For the cakes:
¾ cup plus 1 tbsp. unsalted butter
1¾ cups self-rising flour
heaping 1 cup unrefined superfine sugar
4 eggs
2 tbsp. milk
2 tbsp. ground cinnamon

For the topping:
1 recipe white chocolate buttercream
  (see p. 53)
colored sugar sprinkles

bake: convection 325˚F
conventional 350˚F

1 Line 2 cupcake tins with paper liners or place 24 silicone cupcake liners on a baking sheet. Ensure all the ingredients are at room temperature. Put all the cake ingredients into a large bowl and whisk with an electric mixer 8 to 10 minutes.

2 Spoon the batter into the liners, filling to two-thirds full (a). Bake in the oven 15 minutes until risen and light golden and the cakes spring back when pressed. Remove from the oven and let cool on a wire rack, but still in the tins.

3 Spoon the white chocolate buttercream into a large piping bag fitted with a star tip and pipe swirls of buttercream on each cake. Decorate with the colored sugar sprinkles.

*TO STORE Store in an airtight container and eat within 3 days. Not suitable for freezing.

Tropical Fruit Cake

Straight mixing • For this lighter fruit cake, I have added some sunshine in the form of tropical fruits, including pineapple and mango. This cake is fruity and deliciously moist and nutty to eat. The addition of the chopped marzipan to the cake batter gives a wonderful flavor and texture. I have chosen to finish the cake with a glazed fruit and nut topping, which makes this cake nutritious and easy to make. It is perfect for those who enjoy a good fruit cake without the need to further cover it with marzipan and icing—unless, of course, you are inspired to!

For the cake:

1 cup unsalted butter, plus extra for greasing

$3/4$ cup light brown sugar, lightly packed

6 extra-large eggs, lightly beaten

heaping $3/4$ cup ground almonds

$2 1/4$ cups all-purpose flour

2 tsp. ground ginger

2 tsp. ground cinnamon

1 tsp. baking powder

2 cups golden raisins

heaping $3/4$ cup raisins

$1 1/3$ cups currants

$1/2$ cup naturally colored candied cherries

$1/4$ cup chopped dried mango

$1/4$ cup chopped dried pineapple

$1/4$ cup dark rum

5 oz. marzipan, cut into $1/2$-inch chunks

For the topping:

heaping $1/3$ cup hazelnuts, roughly chopped

heaping $1/3$ cup sliced almonds

$2/3$ cup roughly chopped pecans

$1/2$ cup apricot jam

scant $2/3$ cup brandy

scant $1/4$ cup roughly chopped dried apricots

scant $1/4$ cup roughly chopped dried pineapple

$2/3$ cup roughly chopped naturally colored candied cherries

bake: convection 275°F
conventional 325°F

1 Preheat the oven. Grease and line a deep 8-inch square cake pan with parchment paper or use a nonstick cake pan. Ensure all the ingredients are at room temperature. Place the butter, sugar, eggs, and ground almonds in a bowl and sift in the flour, spices, and baking powder. Beat with an electric mixer 8 to 10 minutes until well mixed, light, and fluffy. Fold in the dried fruits, rum, and chopped marzipan (a).

2 Spoon the batter into the prepared pan, level off the top with the back of a spoon, and bake $1 1/2$ hours until a skewer inserted into the middle of the cake comes out clean. Remove the cake from the oven, but leave the oven on. Leave the cake to cool in the pan and turn out when cold.

3 While the cake is cooling, assemble the topping ingredients (b) and make the topping. Spread out the nuts on a baking sheet and lightly toast in the oven until golden. Remove and let cool.

4 Place the apricot jam and brandy in a medium saucepan and bring gently to the boil, stirring continuously. Remove from the heat and stir in the fruit and toasted nuts until well blended.

5 Spread the topping over the fruit cake and leave about 1 hour to set (c). The cake is now ready to be served (d).

*TO STORE Store up to 2 weeks in an airtight container. Alternatively, wrap the cake in a double layer of waxed paper and foil and place in the freezer up to 1 month.

TIP For the best result, use the moist dried fruit available in the snack packs from most good supermarkets or independent food stores.

a

b

c

d

Heavenly Orange and Strawberry Cake

Whisking • This fresh summery cake is light and airy but less moist than other cakes, as it contains so little butter. Similar in texture to a jelly roll, this cake works well with lashings of fresh crème pâtissière and dressed with white chocolate–dipped strawberries. All you need for the perfect cake for the perfect summer's afternoon.

For the cake:
2 tbsp. unsalted butter, melted and cooled, plus extra for greasing
4 extra-large eggs
heaping ½ cup unrefined superfine sugar
½ cup ground almonds
grated zest of 1 orange
heaping ¾ cup all-purpose flour
1½ tsp. baking powder

For the orange syrup:
scant ⅓ cup unrefined superfine sugar
1 strip orange zest
2 tbsp. Cointreau (optional)

For the filling and topping:
½ recipe crème pâtissière (see p. 55)
1½ cups fresh strawberries, some sliced, some halved, some whole
8 chocolate-dipped strawberries (see p. 60)

bake: convection 275°F
conventional 325°F

1 Preheat the oven. Grease and line a deep 8-inch cake pan with parchment paper or use a nonstick cake pan. Ensure all the ingredients are at room temperature. Whisk together the eggs and sugar with an electric mixer until the mixture thickens, turns pale and leaves a trail (a). This could take 8 to 10 minutes. Fold in the melted butter, ground almonds, and orange zest (b) using a metal spoon. Sift the flour and baking powder into the batter and fold into the batter carefully (c).

2 Transfer the cake batter to the prepared pan and bake 30 to 40 minutes until firm to the touch and a skewer inserted into the middle of the cake comes out clean. Remove from the oven and let cool in the pan 5 minutes before turning out onto a wire rack to cool.

3 To make the orange syrup, place the sugar, orange zest, and scant ½ cup water in a small saucepan and heat gently until dissolved; boil hard 2 to 3 minutes until syrupy. Leave to cool; stir in the Cointreau, if using.

4 When ready to serve, split the cake in half and brush the cut surfaces with the syrup. Place the lower half of the cake on a plate or stand and pour over half the crème pâtissière; cover with most of the sliced strawberries. Add the top half of the cake, pour over the remaining crème pâtissière, and decorate with the remaining strawberries, including the chocolate-dipped ones.

*TO STORE Eat on the day of making, storing it in the refrigerator if necessary, but do not dress with the strawberries until ready to eat.

a

b

c

Fillings and Frostings

Once a cake is baked, it can be further embellished with a host of delicious fillings and frostings. Many of these can be interchanged on different cakes for different occasions. Frostings based on cream or cream cheese should be used only on cakes that can be refrigerated, and should be eaten within two days. Fresh fruit can safely be used as a filling or decoration with these cakes. Buttercreams are stable at room temperature and are therefore perfect for any cakes that need to last a little longer or cannot be refrigerated. Avoid using fresh fruit with buttercream as a filling, as this will ferment at room temperature. Instead, opt for jam or lemon curd.

Chocolate Ganache

Chocolate ganache is the result of combining chocolate with cream to create a rich, velvet-smooth filling or frosting. Served warm, this can be poured over cakes for a wonderful frosting. Once chilled, it begins to thicken and can be used for piping pearls, beads, or scrolls onto cakes (see opposite). It can also be combined with a basic vanilla buttercream (see p. 52) to make a decadent filling for cakes.

1

2

You will need:

½ cup heavy cream

1 cup unsalted butter, diced

1 lb. 2 oz. bittersweet chocolate
(70% cocoa solids), broken into pieces

This makes enough to cover an 8-inch
cake with leftovers for piping.

1 Heat the heavy cream in a heavy saucepan until it begins to boil; remove from the heat. Put the butter and chocolate in a bowl and place over a pan of simmering water to warm gently until just beginning to melt. Alternatively, melt in a microwave. Pour the cream over the butter and chocolate and stir gently to combine.

2 Beat the ganache with a wooden spoon until well combined, rich, and glossy. Use immediately for pouring or allow to thicken for piping (see below). Alternatively, store in an airtight container in the refrigerator up to 2 weeks or freeze 3 months.

POURED GANACHE

1 Cover the top and sides of the cake with a thin layer of buttercream (see p. 52) to seal the crumbs and edges and create a smooth base for the ganache. Chill the cake 30 minutes in the refrigerator or 15 minutes in the freezer.

2 Place the cake on a wire rack over parchment or waxed paper. Warm the ganache (if necessary) in a bowl over a pan of simmering water until glossy and smooth. Ladle it over the top and sides of the cake, using the base of the ladle or a palette knife to smooth it all over. Gently but firmly hold the wire rack and tap sharply onto the countertop to even out the ganache and ensure all areas of the cake are covered.

3 Use a palette knife to lift the cake gently from below to remove it from the rack and place it on a cake board or stand. Let set at room temperature, which may take 2 to 3 hours.

PIPED GANACHE

Ganache will thicken as it cools to room temperature. Beat well until it is firm enough to hold its shape, then spoon into a piping bag fitted with the appropriate icing tip. Note that if the ganache sets too firm in the piping bag or tip, you will need to empty the bag and gently reheat the ganache before filling a fresh bag.

TIP Warm the tip by running it under warm water and drying well before filling the piping bag with ganache. This will help to prevent the ganache from setting in the tip or piping bag.

Buttercream

Any cake you intend to cover with marzipan, icing, or chocolate plastique cannot be refrigerated. Therefore, these cakes cannot be layered with any filling that requires refrigeration. In such cases, buttercream is the perfect solution. This sweet frosting is perfectly stable at room temperature and can be flavored or embellished to create the most delicious flavors to suit all palates and complement a wide range of cake flavors.

You will need:
scant ¾ cup unsalted butter, softened
scant 2½ cups confectioners' sugar, sifted
seeds from 1 vanilla bean

1 Beat the butter in a mixing bowl with an electric mixer 1 minute.

2 Add the confectioners' sugar and beat slowly at first until blended, then on full speed until light and fluffy. Beat in the vanilla seeds (a).

Buttercream will keep up to 2 weeks, stored in the refrigerator. You will need to bring it up to room temperature and beat again until light and fluffy before use.

Variations
Lemon Curd Buttercream
Add a heaping ½ cup lemon curd to one recipe of the basic buttercream (above).

Rose Buttercream
Stir 3 tbsp. rose syrup and a few drops of rose-pink concentrated edible food coloring to the basic buttercream (above).

Orange Buttercream
Add the grated zest of 2 oranges to the basic buttercream (above).

White Chocolate Buttercream
Break 3½ oz. white chocolate into a bowl and melt over simmering water or in a microwave. Cool, then beat into the basic buttercream (opposite) until smooth and glossy (a). This amount will cover 24 cupcakes or fill and cover an 8-inch cake.

Chocolate Ganache Buttercream
Make half a recipe of chocolate ganache (see p. 51) and leave to cool, but not for so long that it sets. Add it to the basic buttercream (opposite) and beat well. Chill until firm, then let the buttercream return to room temperature before beating well again. This can be stored in an airtight container in the refrigerator up to 2 weeks. This amount will cover 24 cupcakes or fill and cover an 8-inch cake.

Crème Pâtissière

You will need:
6 extra-large egg yolks
1 tbsp. vanilla extract
²/₃ cup superfine sugar
scant ½ cup all-purpose flour, sifted
scant 2½ cups milk
2 tbsp. butter, diced
generous ½ cup heavy cream
1 lb. 2 oz. crème fraîche

Crème pâtissière is a deliciously fresh creamy custard that works very well with light cakes, especially if you want to turn them into a dessert. It will keep up to 2 days in the refrigerator. Once served, it should be eaten within 4 hours.

1 Put the egg yolks, vanilla extract, and superfine sugar into a large mixing bowl. Whisk with an electric mixer until pale and thick.

2 Whisk in the flour until it is all incorporated.

3 Bring the milk to the boil in a heavy saucepan and gradually pour it into the egg mixture (decanting it first into a pitcher, if this is easier), whisking continuously.

4 Return the custard to the saucepan and cook over gentle heat, stirring continuously, until thick and glossy. Continue to cook 2 minutes more, stirring continuously; remove from the heat and beat in the butter.

5 Pour the crème pâtissière into a clean bowl and cover with plastic wrap, ensuring the wrap rests on the surface of the custard. Chill in the refrigerator. Whip the cream until firm (being careful not to overwhip it) and stir carefully into the cooled custard.

6 Stir in the crème fraîche just before serving. Use as a filling and/or topping.

*TO STORE Can be kept chilled at stage 5 up to 2 days.

Cream Cheese Frostings

Cream cheese frostings have a strong affinity with cakes. The combination of full-fat cream cheese (ideally mascarpone) with sugar and additional flavors provides a variety of rich sweet frostings. More stable than whipped cream yet not as rich as buttercream, a cream cheese frosting is the perfect partner to many afternoon teatime cakes.

You will need:
2¼ cups mascarpone cheese
⅓ cup unrefined superfine sugar

Beat the mascarpone and sugar together until light and fluffy.

Variations
Orange Cream Cheese Frosting
Add the zest of 2 oranges and 5 drops of orange oil to the basic recipe (above).

Vanilla Cream Cheese Frosting
Add the seeds of one vanilla bean or 1 tsp. vanilla extract to the basic recipe (above).

Coffee Cream Cheese Frosting
Beat the mascarpone and sugar together (a). Dissolve 3 tbsp. instant coffee in 3 tbsp. boiling water. Let cool, then add to the basic recipe (above) (b). Whisk until combined (c). Use as desired (d).

a

b

c

d

Lime Frosting

Zesty lime and creamy coconut make the perfect frosting for filling or topping teatime cakes.

You will need:
grated zest and juice of 2 limes
3½ oz. creamed coconut, grated
heaping ⅓ cup unsalted butter, softened
scant 1½ cups confectioners' sugar, sifted

1 Mix together the lime zest and juice and the creamed coconut. Microwave or place over a pan of simmering water until the coconut melts, then let cool.

2 Beat the butter until smooth and creamy using an electric mixer. Add the confectioners' sugar and whisk slowly at first, then at full speed, until light and fluffy. Stir in the cooled coconut and lime mixture and whisk until light and fluffy.

Glacé Icing

This classic frosting combines confectioners' sugar with water, which may be colored and flavored. Popular flavors are lemon, coffee, and chocolate (see below). The icing should be mixed to a fairly runny consistency and is generally drizzled into position over large cakes, cupcakes, tarts, and buns, placed on a wire rack with a sheet of parchment or waxed paper underneath to catch the excess icing. Alternatively, it can be spooned over the top and sides of a cake. Let set 15 minutes before transferring to a plate ready to decorate. It will set to the touch, but will not set firm like royal icing. As a result, it can be spooned into a piping bag and the end snipped to pipe very simple messages and line decoration, but cannot hold its shape, like royal icing, for more intricate piped decoration. The quantities listed here will be sufficient to decorate 24 cupcakes or cover one 6- to 8-inch round larger cake. Once in place, the icing will last up to 2 weeks (usually longer than the cake itself!). Any remaining glacé icing should be discarded.

Lemon Glacé Icing

You will need:
juice of 2 lemons (strained to remove any seeds and pulp)
4 cups confectioners' sugar, sifted

1 Pour the lemon juice into a medium bowl and add the confectioners' sugar a spoonful at a time, stirring well to remove any lumps.

2 Gently stir the sugar and juice together until you achieve a white icing that is no longer translucent but is still glossy and not dry or stiff. Spoon, pour, or spread over cakes as required.

Variations
Coffee Glacé Icing

4 cups confectioners' sugar, sifted
2 tsp. instant coffee dissolved in ¼ cup boiling water

Follow the method for Lemon Glacé Icing (above), replacing the lemon juice with the coffee mixture.

Chocolate Glacé Icing

4 cups confectioners' sugar, sifted
1 tbsp. unsweetened cocoa powder dissolved in ¼ cup boiling water

Follow the method for Lemon Glacé Icing (above), replacing the lemon juice with the cocoa mixture.

TIP Glacé icing adds a lot of moisture, sweetness, and flavor to cakes, which makes it perfect for the straight mixing baked cakes. The technique is less complicated than other toppings, so a great recipe for beginners or children.

You will need:

bar of chocolate, at room temperature

Chocolate Curls

These chocolate curls are a very simple standby for an effective decoration. They can be used to decorate large cakes, individual cakes, or even ice cream. Use these decorations as soon as you have created them, as they tend to break up if stored.

1 Hold the bar of chocolate in one hand and the vegetable peeler in the other, then carefully but purposefully pull the peeler along the full length of the edge of the chocolate bar.

2 The chocolate curls will fall onto the countertop. Use a palette knife to gather them up carefully into a small bowl.

TIP The chocolate must be at room temperature for the peeler to run smoothly. If the chocolate is chilled or too cold, it will be brittle and the chocolate will not form nice curls.

You will need:

7 oz. white chocolate drops

2⅔ cups (about 20) strawberries, clean and dry but not chilled

Chocolate-Dipped Strawberries

Chocolate-dipped strawberries are the epitome of luxury and decadence for a special occasion. Dipping strawberries in smooth white chocolate (or milk or dark, if you prefer) makes the perfect decoration for a summer party cake—either served as part of the decoration or accompanying the cake to dress the plate. The white chocolate will have to be tempered (a process of heating and cooling the chocolate to ensure it is precrystallized and sets with a shiny gloss finish and a clean "snap" bite). This is done here using a much simpler method than usual, but one that achieves good results at home.

1 Put half the chocolate drops in a heatproof bowl set over a saucepan of gently simmering water and leave until the chocolate melts. Remove the pan from the heat. (Alternatively, put the bowl in a microwave and heat on full power 1 minute until melted.) Add the remaining chocolate drops to the melted chocolate a handful at a time and stir with a wooden spoon. This brings the temperature of the chocolate down—a vital part of the tempering process.

2 Stir with the wooden spoon until you feel the chocolate thicken slightly and move around the bowl with a definite "clack," and until it coats the back of the wooden spoon with a glossy sheen that holds.

3 Hold each strawberry by the green calyx and dip into the white chocolate. Hold it there for a few seconds, then lift the strawberry out. Gently drag the strawberry on the side of the bowl to remove the excess chocolate.

4 Place it on a sheet of waxed paper to set at room temperature. Dip the remaining strawberries in the same way.

TIP The strawberries must be at room temperature, otherwise they will chill the white chocolate too quickly, which will affect the tempering. Chocolate-dipped fruit must be eaten the same day, otherwise the fruit will shrink away from the chocolate. Do not refrigerate chocolate-dipped fruit, as the chocolate will sweat as it comes back up to room temperature with the fruit.

4

Careful Covering and Stacking

In this chapter I will show you how to cover a variety of shapes and sizes of cakes with marzipan, rolled fondant, chocolate plastique, and royal icing. A flawless covering is fundamental to having the perfect canvas on which to decorate your cakes. Don't worry if your cakes are not perfect when starting out, as many undulations, bumps, and bulges can be masked when you add the decoration later on. However, do practice on a dummy tier of Styrofoam, if possible, as it can really help to build your confidence. Once your cakes are covered, I will show you how to dowel and stack them successfully so they are secure, safe, and even.

Note that cakes covered with marzipan and icing or chocolate plastique cannot be refrigerated once covered, as the icing or chocolate will pick up moisture in the refrigerator, which would adversely affect the texture.

TIPS Always wear a plain white cotton t-shirt when working, so that any fibers that land in the icing (you'd be surprised!) don't show up. Also, ensure you have all the equipment you need at hand, including a clean damp cloth, and sharpen your knife to give it a really clean edge. I like to work with a silicone rolling pin rather than a wood or marble one, as the former can impart a grain effect and the latter can affect the temperature of the covering.

Marzipan

The role of marzipan as a base coat is threefold:

- It gives the cake a really firm, smooth foundation on which to apply the top coat of rolled fondant, chocolate plastique, or royal icing.
- It is oil based (being made from almonds), which means it is perfect for locking in moisture, helping to keep cakes moist.
- It will mask the color of the cake bleeding through to the icing.

For a single-tier birthday cake, which may be served and eaten within 2 to 3 days of baking, it is not essential to cover it with marzipan first. I would, however, cover it with two thinner layers of rolled fondant.

For a multitiered wedding cake, however, it is essential to have the initial layer of marzipan to ensure the cakes are firm and can support the dowels.

For fresher cakes (such as chocolate, vanilla, and lemon), you could replace the marzipan with a base coat of white chocolate plastique before adding the top coat.

Rolled fondant

Rolled fondant is a sweet icing rolled out like marzipan, used as the top coat for many celebration cakes, and for lining boards. It is available commercially in a variety of colors, although white, ivory, and chocolate are the most popular. Made from sugar, glucose syrup, water, and a little vegetable oil, it covers beautifully and dries to a firm, smooth finish with a soft sheen, and can easily be cut with a knife. It is the perfect canvas for further decoration, including hand piping, molding, and painting, as it is less porous than royal icing. It can be stored safely in a sealed plastic bag up to 12 months and should be kneaded with minimal confectioners' sugar until it is pliable and soft but not sticky.

BRUSHING WITH ALCOHOL
Cakes to be covered with rolled fondant should have a base coat of marzipan, rolled fondant, or chocolate plastique, which should be brushed with brandy or other alcohol before the rolled fondant top coat is applied. This reacts gently with the sugar in the base coat, forming a sticky glue for the rolled fondant to adhere to. The alcohol acts as an antiseptic to help prevent mold growth between the marzipan and fondant layers, which is of particular concern on a fruit cake, which

may be covered and decorated some considerable time before the celebration. This is less likely for freshly baked sponge cakes, as they are generally prepared within a week of the celebration and eaten soon after. There is little flavor added to the cake itself, so this is not a major concern for children's cakes. However, you can use cooled boiled water instead. Note that using boiled jam, as for attaching marzipan, is unsuitable here: It is too viscous and creates lumps.

Chocolate plastique

Chocolate plastique is malleable, yet sets firm and can be used to make hand-molded roses, cut-out leaves, and collars and fans for helter-skelter-style cakes (see p. 164). The roses, leaves, and fans can be made up to 3 months in advance and stored in an airtight container at room temperature. They are perfect decorations for finishing individual cakes, adding to poured ganache chocolate cakes, or adorning majestic wedding cakes.

Chocolate plastique on its own can be rather chewy, so it is best to mix it 1:1 with white or chocolate rolled fondant when using it to cover cakes. White chocolate plastique (see p. 74) is the perfect base coat for sponge cakes, such as vanilla, lemon, or chocolate, as an alternative to marzipan. It creates a good base for a top coat of white or dark chocolate plastique (see p. 75), or rolled fondant. Follow the instructions for covering cakes with rolled fondant.

Chocolate-covered and decorated cakes tend to be less formal, less refined, and more sculptural than iced cakes, with real wow factor. They can be easier to make, as many of the components are made ahead. However, cakes covered with a top coat of chocolate plastique will be more susceptible to temperature fluctuations. They will be very stable under the right conditions but will be badly affected by moisture, humidity, and direct sunlight.

As a rule of thumb:

- Cakes should not be refrigerated: They are quite happy at room temperature.
- Cakes should not be allowed to get wet (avoid carrying these cakes to and from party venues in the rain, unless well covered).
- Cakes will droop if the humidity is high—which is of particular concern in tents with no air conditioning.
- Cakes should not be placed in direct sunlight, as this will cause the chocolate to melt.

Covering individual cakes

All individual cakes smaller than 4 inches should be cut out of one larger cake. This ensures that each cake is consistent in size and evenly baked and moist. I tend to bake 8-inch square cakes, 3 inches deep, which I cut in half horizontally, then cut out twenty-five 1½-inch square cakes from each layer (so 50 in total), or sixteen 2-inch round cakes (so 32 in total). If the cakes are to be filled, I cut the cake in half horizontally, as before, then split and fill each half with buttercream before cutting out the cakes. There will be less waste from individual square cakes compared with round, though the trimmings from the latter can make the base of a delicious trifle. Individual cakes can be covered with marzipan and rolled fondant, as I will show you here, but the method would be the same if you were covering with white or dark chocolate plastique (see p. 74). Regardless of whether the top coat of chocolate is white, dark, or combined, I always recommend that the base coat be white chocolate plastique.

Covering individual square cakes

Cut each cake layer into 5 strips and then cut each strip into 5 squares, each measuring 1½ inches.

1 Knead the marzipan until smooth and pliable. This is a two-handed operation—one hand gently draws the outside to the center while the other hand keeps the ball moving in a clockwise direction.

2 Dust the countertop liberally with confectioners' sugar to prevent sticking. Use a rolling pin in short, sharp strokes in one direction only.

3 Lift the marzipan with a quarter turn and repeat rolling until it reaches the desired size and a thickness of ⅛ inch. Do not turn the marzipan over.

4 Use a pizza wheel to cut the marzipan into 4-inch squares.

TIP The pizza wheel is a rotary cutter, and, as such, will not pull or snag the marzipan.

5 Brush each individual square cake with boiled, sieved apricot jam, using a pastry brush.

6 Lay one square of marzipan over the cake.

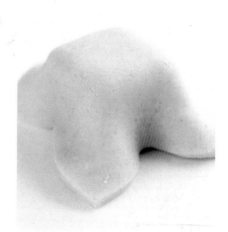

7 Let the marzipan fall down around the sides of the cake.

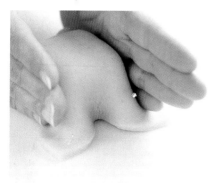

8 Shape the marzipan over the top and sides with your hands.

9 Use 2 straight-edged smoothers to press the marzipan onto the top and sides of the cake to create a neat cube shape.

10 Use a sharp knife to trim all the edges straight at the base of the cake. It is now ready to be iced.

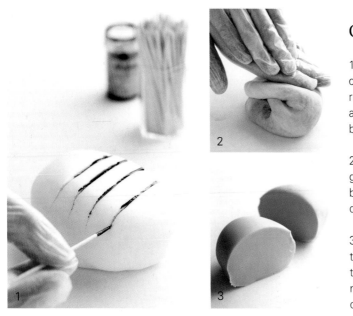

Coloring rolled fondant

1 To blend your own color of rolled fondant, use concentrated edible food colorings. Start with the required amount of white or ivory rolled fondant and gently draw a toothpick dipped in one or a blend of colors across the rolled fondant.

2 Wearing disposable latex or plastic gloves, gently knead the paste as described on p. 66, building up the color(s) until you reach the desired color and intensity.

3 The only way to check if the color is uniform throughout the entire piece of rolled fondant is to cut it in half with a sharp knife. If there is any marbling effect, continue kneading until the color is even.

Covering individual square cakes with rolled fondant

1 Brush the top and sides of the marzipan-covered cake with brandy.

2 Roll out the rolled fondant and cut into 4-inch squares using a pizza wheel. Lay one square of rolled fondant over the cake.

3 Shape the rolled fondant over the top and sides with your hands.

4 Use 2 straight-edged smoothers to press the rolled fondant onto the sides of the cake.

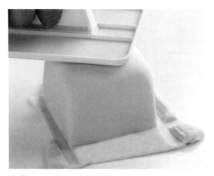

5 Press the rolled fondant down on the top of the cake, too, to create a square shape.

6 Use a sharp knife to trim the edges straight at the base of the cake. It is now ready to be decorated.

Covering individual round cakes

Round cakes use 3 concentric circular cutters: 2-inch for the cake, 2½-inch for the marzipan base coat, and 2¾-inch for the rolled fondant top coat.

1 Cut out the cakes with the 2-inch cutter and brush with boiled, sieved apricot jam. If preferred, cut the cake layer into 4 strips first, then stamp out the cakes.

2 Roll out the marzipan and cut it into squares as for individual square cakes. Lay a square over a cake and shape to fit the top and sides with your hands. Use the 2½-inch cutter over the top of the cake to trim and remove the excess marzipan.

3 Brush with brandy and repeat with the rolled fondant. Place the 2¾-inch cutter over the top of the cake to remove the excess rolled fondant.

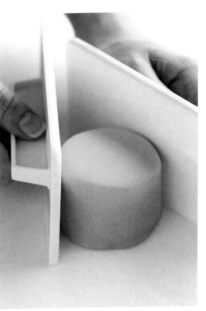

4 Use 2 straight-edged smoothers in a gentle rotation motion to flatten, shape, and smooth the cake. The cake is now ready for decoration.

TIP These individual cakes will handle better if they are chilled prior to being brushed with jam.

Covering large cakes

Cakes that are going to be decorated should be covered with two layers: a base coat of marzipan, white chocolate plastique, or rolled fondant, and a flawless top coat of royal icing, rolled fondant, or chocolate plastique. If you want to top-coat the cake with royal icing, apply panels of marzipan, rolled fondant, or white chocolate plastique to the top and sides of a square cake separately (or a top panel and a large collar to go all around, for a round cake) to retain the sharp edges and give a crisp finish (see below). If you want to top-coat a round or square cake with any other covering, the base coat should be rolled out and laid over the cake in one sheet to give the cake a lovely rounded finish (see opposite).

Applying a base coat for a crisp, angular finish

1 Invert the cake on to a cake board, usually 3 inches larger than the cake, and ice into position in the center of the board. Plug any gaps around the bottom with pieces of the base coat. Note: Cakes that are to be royal-iced sit on a large cake board rather than a same-size board (see opposite).

2 Brush the top of the cake with boiled, sieved apricot jam. Roll out the base coat and cut a piece to fit the top of the cake. You can use a ruler, cake pan, or cake board for this. Lift the base coat top into position and gently tease it out to fit to the edges.

3 Use 2 straight-edged smoothers to neaten these edges so they are flush with the sides of the cake.

4 Brush the sides of the cake with more jam. Roll out more of the base coat and cut panels for the sides. Press one side in place.

5 Trim with a sharp knife as needed to achieve a flush finish, then add the remaining panels. (If you are covering a round cake, fix the large collar into position all round.)

Applying a base coat for a smooth, rounded finish

1 Knead the marzipan/rolled fondant/white chocolate plastique until smooth and pliable, as described on p. 66. Liberally dust the countertop with confectioners' sugar and roll out the base coat to the desired size and thickness. Brush the cake (which, because it is not going to be royal iced, should already be on a cake board of the same size) with boiled, sieved apricot jam. Lift the base coat with both hands right underneath it so it rests over your hands, wrists, and lower arms. Focus on the center of the base coat and note the center of the cake. Lift the base coat over the top of the cake and when the center is directly over the center of the cake, gently release the base coat from the center outward, removing your arms carefully to allow the base coat to fall into position over the cake. In this way, there is no stress applied to the base coat. It is not being pulled or forced over any edge of the cake or on a rolling pin and should have even length to cover all the sides.

2 Use your hands to cup the base coat over the sides of the cake to the base. For a square cake, tease the base coat over the corners of the cake first, gently skirting the base coat out to avoid any folds.

3 Use a straight-edged smoother to smooth the base coat over the top and sides of the cake to create a flat top and smooth sides.

4 Lift the cake on its board and continue to run around the sides with the smoother, encouraging the base coat down below the cake board. This will help you to create really straight sides and a perfect round base. Insert a sharp knife below the cake board, with the blade away from you, and cut the excess base coat away from the cake, pressing against and away from the cake board.

GUIDE TO QUANTITIES TO COVER CAKES WITH MARZIPAN/CHOCOLATE PLASTIQUE														● round cake ■ square cake	
size of cake	4-inch ●	4-inch ■	6-inch ●	6-inch ■	8-inch ●	8-inch ■	9-inch ●	9-inch ■	10-inch ●	10-inch ■	12-inch ●	12-inch ■	14-inch ●	14-inch ■	16-inch ●	16-inch ■
quantity	14 oz.	1 lb. 2 oz.	1 lb. 5 oz.	1 lb. 10 oz.	1 lb. 12 oz.	2 lb. 4 oz.	2 lb. 4 oz.	2 lb. 12 oz.	2 lb. 12 oz.	3 lb. 5 oz.	3 lb. 14 oz.	4 lb. 8 oz.	5 lb.	5 lb. 13 oz.	6 lb. 4 oz.	6 lb. 9 oz.

Applying a rolled fondant top coat on a round cake

1

2

3

1 Knead the rolled fondant until smooth and pliable but not sticky. Brush the top and sides of the cake with brandy or cooled boiled water (not the jam used for the base coat). Roll out the rolled fondant on a countertop lightly dusted with confectioners' sugar to the desired size and thickness, then drape it over the cake as described on p. 71.

2 Use your hands to smooth and stick the icing over the top and sides of the cake.

3 Run over the top and sides of the cake with plastic smoothers (rounded for the top, straight-edged for the sides) until the rolled fondant is completely smooth. Lift the cake on its cake board and use a sharp

knife at eye level to trim the excess rolled fondant away from you against the cake board. The cake is now ready to be decorated.

TIP It can be easier to set the cake on a turntable to trim the excess rolled fondant—as long as the turntable is smaller than the cake itself. Alternatively, use an overturned bowl.

How to avoid rolled fondant cracking

1 Make sure you knead it thoroughly so that it is warmed, malleable, and pliable, but not sticky.
2 Add only a light dusting of confectioners' sugar at the kneading stage to prevent it from drying out.
3 Roll out no thinner than $\frac{1}{6}$-inch thick.
4 Add a second layer for a smoother finish and to avoid cracking over angular edges.
5 Handle the rolled fondant lightly, lifting it gently, and draping it over the top and sides of a cake, rather than stretching it.

GUIDE TO QUANTITIES TO COVER CAKES WITH ROLLED FONDANT															● round cake ■ square cake
size of cake	6-inch ●	6-inch ■	8-inch ●	8-inch ■	9-inch ●	9-inch ■	10-inch ●	10-inch ■	12-inch ●	12-inch ■	14-inch ●	14-inch ■	16-inch ●	16-inch ■
quantity	1 lb. 10 oz.	1 lb. 14 oz.	2 lb. 4 oz.	2 lb. 12 oz.	2 lb. 12 oz.	3 lb. 5 oz.	3 lb. 5 oz.	4 lb.	4 lb. 12 oz.	5 lb. 3 oz.	6 lb.	6 lb. 9 oz.	7 lb. 2 oz.	7 lb. 11 oz.

GUIDE TO QUANTITIES TO COVER CAKE BOARDS WITH ROLLED FONDANT/CHOCOLATE PLASTIQUE																
size of board	7-inch ●	7-inch ■	8-inch ●	8-inch ■	9-inch ●	9-inch ■	10-inch ●	10-inch ■	11-inch ●	11-inch ■	12-inch ●	12-inch ■	13-inch ●	13-inch ■	14-inch ●	14-inch ■
quantity	11 oz.	14 oz.	15 oz.	1 lb. 3 oz.	1 lb. 4 oz.	1 lb. 8 oz.	1 lb. 7 oz.	1 lb. 13 oz.	1 lb. 12 oz.	2 lb. 4 oz.	2 lb. 2 oz.	2 lb. 11 oz.	2 lb. 11 oz.	2 lb. 2 oz.	3 lb.	3 lb. 8 oz.

size of board	15-inch ●	15-inch ■	16-inch ●	16-inch ■	18-inch ●	18-inch ■	20-inch ●	20-inch ■	22-inch ●	22-inch ■
quantity	3 lb. 5 oz.	4 lb. 3 oz.	3 lb. 12 oz.	4 lb. 12 oz.	4 lb. 14 oz.	6 lb.	5 lb. 12 oz.	7 lb. 4 oz.	7 lb.	9 lb.

Covering (lining) a cake board with rolled fondant

A cake looks professionally finished if the cake board is also lined with rolled fondant or chocolate plastique and edged in a double satin or grosgrain ribbon. Boards should be lined the day before the cakes are covered, to give them sufficient time to dry out overnight and make them easier to handle.

1 Brush the cake board with water. Knead the rolled fondant until smooth and pliable, then roll out on a confectioners' sugar–dusted countertop to ⅛-inch thick. Lift and place over the cake board from the center outward. Use a straight-edged smoother to even and smooth the rolled fondant over the cake board.

2 Lift the board and use a sharp knife to trim the excess rolled fondant by cutting against the board away from you. The edge of the cake board should now be covered with some complementary ribbon of the correct width, fixed in place with a little glue.

3 Once the cake is covered, spread a little royal icing in the center of the board to hold it.

4 Use 2 hands to hold the cake from underneath and gently set the cake down into position on the cake board. Use 2 plastic straight-edged smoothers to nudge the cake so it is centrally positioned and smoothed against the cake board. The cake is now ready to be decorated.

TIP Ensure your knife is really sharp, and clean it between each trim for a really clean, professional finish. Leave the cake to dry overnight.

Making glitter boards

For added glamor and a sense of occasion, it can be fun to cover cake boards with a different-colored rolled fondant and add edible glitter. This is a great way to create the impression of a larger cake and to incorporate glitter that won't actually be eaten.

1 Cover the board as described above, using a colored rolled fondant of your choice. Lay the board on a large sheet of waxed paper. Spray the covered board with edible varnish or brush with sugar glue.

2 Liberally dredge the cake board with edible glitter in a complementary color. Wait a few moments before shaking off the excess. Let firm overnight.

Chocolate Plastique

Chocolate plastique is a soft, pliable paste made from chocolate, glucose syrup, and stock syrup. It can be rolled out like marzipan but has all the taste of chocolate. It can be bought from specialist cake-decorating stores or made at home.

Plastique Stock Syrup

You will need:
2/3 cup superfine sugar
1/3 cup glucose syrup

Yields scant 2 cups

Place the sugar, glucose syrup and 1 cup water (a) in a saucepan and bring to a boil. Remove from the heat and leave to cool.

This recipe will provide slightly more than is required for the white chocolate plastique recipe here.

TIP Make chocolate plastique in large batches, as it will keep happily at room temperature for up to 3 months. Begin preparing the plastique at least 1 week before you need it, as it can take some time to set. For milk chocolate plastique, mix equal quantities of white and dark together.

White Chocolate Plastique

You will need:
3 lb. 12 oz. white chocolate buttons
4 oz. cocoa butter buttons
1 2/3 cups glucose syrup
1 1/4 cups plastique stock syrup (left)

Yields 5 lb. 8 oz.

1 Melt the chocolate buttons in a microwave or in a large heat-proof bowl placed over a pan of simmering water. Melt the cocoa butter buttons in a separate bowl. Once they have both melted, mix them together and stir well. (Their different melting points mean that they need to be melted separately. Both need to be melted completely, but not overheated, for this recipe to work.)

2 Measure the glucose syrup and stock syrup together in a clean bowl and warm in the microwave. (This brings the temperature up to similar to that of the white chocolate.)

3 Pour the chocolate mixture over the glucose and stock syrup (b) and mix with a wooden spoon until smooth. It should cling to the spoon and leave the sides of the bowl clean (c).

4 Transfer into a large freezer bag and spread the paste out so that as much surface area touches the bag as possible. This will speed up the setting process. Leave overnight and then for up to 3 days to set firm. The chocolate plastique can now be stored at room temperature for up to 3 months, if required.

5 When ready to use, turn the bag inside out and peel it away from the plastique. Knead until smooth and pliable. If the paste is really soft, due to a warm room, add confectioners' sugar until it thickens and is smooth. If it is really firm, due to a cold room, microwave it for 10 seconds at a time until it softens and is malleable.

a

b

c

Dark Chocolate Plastique

You will need:

2 lb. 12 oz. semisweet chocolate buttons (maximum 55% cocoa solids)

1 lb. 9 oz. glucose syrup

Yields 4 lb.

1 Melt the chocolate in a microwave or in a large heat-resistant bowl placed over a saucepan of simmering water. Leave to cool slightly.

2 Heat the glucose syrup in a pan or a microwave so it is at a similar temperature to the chocolate. Pour into a large bowl (a).

3 Gradually beat the chocolate into the glucose syrup, beating it to a thick paste that leaves the sides of the bowl clean (b). Transfer to a large freezer bag and leave overnight to set. Store at room temperature up to 3 months.

4 When ready to use, turn the bag inside out and peel away from the plastique. Knead until smooth and pliable. If the paste is really firm, microwave 10 seconds at a time until it softens and is malleable.

TIP Using semisweet chocolate with maximum 55% cocoa solids prevents the paste from breaking and being too bitter.

a

b

Royal Icing

Royal icing combines fresh egg white with confectioners' sugar and a little lemon juice to create a rich, thick, glossy icing that can be used to cover cakes, add additional elaborate piping or be used for run-outs. The albumen (protein) in egg white gives the icing its elasticity and viscosity, and enables it to set firm once dried. The lemon juice strengthens the egg white and gives the icing a pleasant taste. Once a batch of royal icing has been made, it can be stored safely in a sealed airtight container for up to 7 days if kept cool and dry. Beat the icing well each time before use. The standard recipe, which is ideal for piping, can have glycerine added to it to give a softer set, making it ideal for covering. Alternatively, it can have water added to make a flooding icing (see p. 79).

You will need:

1 extra-large egg white, at room
   temperature

3²/₃ cups (approx.) confectioners' sugar,
   sifted

½ lemon, cut into wedges

1 Assemble the ingredients.

2 Put the egg white in a large and
very clean bowl.

3 Whisk on full speed until it reaches
the soft peak stage.

4 Add two-thirds of the confectioners'
sugar and whisk slowly at first, then
on full speed for 2 minutes.

5 Continue to add the confectioners'
sugar until the icing resembles
freshly whipped heavy cream. It
should have a firm peak but still be
glossy—not grainy or powdery. It
should be fluffy, like meringue. (You
may not need all the sugar.)

6 Squeeze the lemon wedges through
a strainer (to remove any seeds and
the fleshy pulp) into the icing. Whisk
for 1 minute more. The icing is now
ready to use for piping.

Royal Icing for Covering

Add 1 tsp. glycerine to the icing
and whisk for 1 minute more. The
glycerine allows the royal icing to
retain some softness as it sets once
it has been spread over the cake.
This makes it smoother and less
brittle, and easier to cut. Do not
attempt to use this icing for piping,
as it has a tendency to crumble.

You will need these quantities:

For a 6-inch cake: 2 recipes

For a 8-inch cake: 2½ recipes

For a 10-inch cake: 3 recipes

For a 12-inch cake: 4 recipes

Applying a royal icing top coat

I devised this method for covering cakes with royal icing to deal with a number of modern-day issues—how to royal-ice a sponge cake for it to remain fresh for a celebration; and how to have the appearance and taste of royal icing with the ease of cutting of rolled fondant. Here is the solution. The cake is first covered with panels of rolled fondant, and just one final top coat of royal icing is applied to seal the cake and give the all-important royal-iced finish. This method is much less time consuming than building up a number of layers of royal icing to achieve the desired thickness, so it can be used for fresh sponge cakes baked and iced much closer to the celebration. This technique also ensures the cake will still cut beautifully, as there is only one thin coat of royal icing over a rolled fondant base. A thicker layer of royal icing tends to be hard and brittle.

1 Follow the process on p. 70, using panels of rolled fondant instead of marzipan. (If you are using a round cake, cut one large collar and fix into position all round the sides.)

2 Make a batch of fresh royal icing with glycerine (see p. 77). Starting on the top, use a palette knife to spread sufficient icing over the cake, using a paddling motion to smooth and remove excess air bubbles.

3 Hold an icing ruler at a 45-degree angle and, slowly but smoothly, draw the ruler toward you to create a smooth final top coat of icing. This process can be repeated a number of times until you are happy with the finish. Trim the edges with a sharp knife. Leave to set at least 4 hours or overnight.

4 For a square cake, spread the icing over two opposite sides first. Then, using a royal-ice metal scraper and holding it at a 45-degree angle in contact with the cake board, draw the scraper smoothly toward you. Repeat on the other two sides.

For a round cake, place it on a turntable. Hold the scraper against the side of the cake and, with the other hand, turn the turntable one full circle (revolution) in a smooth motion. This will give a clean finish all the way around the cake.

5 Trim the top and sides with a sharp knife, and leave to set for 4 hours or overnight. Finally, use a palette knife to apply royal icing to the cake board and use the scraper to smooth all the way around. Use a sharp knife to trim away the excess against the cake board. (Again, a round cake can have the board covered on a turntable for ease.) Leave to set for at least 4 hours or overnight. The iced cake is now ready to be decorated.

Stacking

Whichever method of stacking you choose, make sure that you use only those cakes that are firm and have set properly; that all tiers are placed on thick cake boards first; and that the plastic doweling rods (which are removed when the cake is cut) are cut and trimmed evenly. Use more rods for softer or heavier cakes to provide maximum support. To dowel and stack a number of tiers, dowel each tier separately first before assembling the entire cake when instructed, fixing the tiers into position with royal icing. Check from all sides that the cake is evenly placed on the tier below. Let each tier set 15 minutes before proceeding with the next tier. Finally, use a spirit level to ensure the base table and tiers are even as you assemble a cake (especially useful if setting up a cake in a tent).

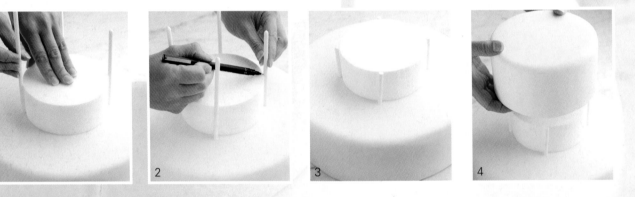

Blocking

You will need:

2-inch or 3-inch deep Styrofoam block, round or square, depending on the shape of the tiers, 4 inches smaller than the dimension of the lower tier

4 doweling rods per tier for cakes up to and including 10 inches in diameter, and 8 rods per tier for cakes larger than that

marker pen

ruler

sharp heavy-duty scissors

spirit level

Blocking is the name for tiers that have been stacked with a Styrofoam block between them to be filled with sugar or fresh flowers. This is a more contemporary style than traditional pillars, and creates additional height, as well as contributing to the overall design. I recommend a 2-inch) gap between tiers for a single row of flowers and 3 inches for a double row. With this technique, it is essential to cut each doweling rod to the height of the Styrofoam block used between the tiers (plus the height of the cake below). The block adds surface area and a medium into which to insert wired fresh or sugar flowers and ribbons. The rods support the tiers and hold the Styrofoam block securely in position, which means it does not need to be iced into position.

1 Place the base tier on a level countertop and position the Styrofoam block in the center of the cake. Hold the block with one hand and gently but firmly insert the doweling rods evenly spaced around the outside up against the block. Push them all the way to the base of the cake until they reach the cake board.

2 Use a marker pen to mark on the inside of each dowel where it is level with the Styrofoam block.

3 Remove all the dowels carefully. Lay them down and line them up against a level edge, and mark one clear line using the marker pen and the ruler across the average height. This will level the surface for the next tier if this tier is uneven. Cut each doweling rod with heavy-duty scissors at the marked line, then hold them all together on a flat surface to check they are all even. Trim if necessary. Reinsert all the doweling rods.

4 Place the next tier into position. The tier should be stable and firm and not wobble. If it does wobble, remove all the doweling rods, trim each by $1/8$ inch, check they are all even, then reinsert. The upper tier should now sit firmly in position. Repeat for further tiers.

Direct stacking

You will need:

6 doweling rods per tier
ruler
marker pen
sharp heavy-duty scissors
spirit level

Stacking tiers directly on top of one another is the safest method to stack cakes and creates the illusion of one large cake. This is the perfect solution for cakes that have to be transported some distance.

1 Place the base tier on a level countertop and insert the first doweling rod in the center of the cake, pushing it down until it reaches the cake board. Use a pen to mark the dowel in line with the top of the cake. Remove the dowel carefully. Lay and line up this dowel with 5 others so the mark is clearly visible. Place a ruler across the dowels at the mark and use a marker pen to mark the other 5 dowels at the same position. Cut each doweling rod with heavy-duty scissors at the marked line, then hold them all together on a flat surface to check they are all even. Trim if necessary.

2 Insert the dowels into the cake, making sure they remain within the base area of the next tier (offset, if relevant). Push them all the way down until they reach the board.

3 Spread a small amount of royal icing onto the surface of the cake over the rods to fix the next tier into position.

4 Place the upper tier in position.

Stacking with a central column

You will need:

ribbon for Styrofoam block,
   1-inch wide
glue stick
6 doweling rods per tier
1-inch deep Styrofoam
   block, round or square,
   depending on the shape
   of the tiers, 4 inches
   smaller than the
   dimension of the base tier
ruler
marker pen
sharp heavy-duty scissors
spirit level

Central columns made from Styrofoam add additional height to a tiered cake. Wrap in a complementing ribbon, fixed with glue. They are clearly visible, so the doweling rods have to be concealed beneath the Styrofoam block. This method is less stable than stacking or blocking, so should be recommended only on smaller cakes and never in a tent, where a stable floor cannot be guaranteed!

Follow steps 1–2 of the direct stacking method, making sure the dowels remain within the base area of the Styrofoam block to go on top.

3 Spread a small amount of royal icing onto the surface of the cake over the doweling rods and fix the central column into position.

4 Check that the column is central and even with a spirit level. Leave to set for 15 minutes, then place the next tier on top. Repeat for more tiers, as necessary, letting each column set in between.

Master Class

In this chapter I am going to show you the tricks of my trade. These will enable you to build up your own repertoire of intricate decorations that can be applied to so many cake designs. The master class will include hand piping, hand molding, hand painting, cutters, and ribbons. Many of these techniques are relatively simple, yet effective to achieve, making them relevant to a commercial market and the time-strapped cake decorator. Beautiful wired flowers can look stunning, but they are painstaking and lengthy to make. I have therefore made a conscious decision not to include these in this book, focusing more on a larger number of less time-consuming techniques. You will find cakes featuring all these general techniques in the Cake Gallery (pp. 116–211).

Hand piping

Hand piping is an instant and gratifying technique used to decorate cakes. From creating a simple hand-piped message to more elaborate basket-weaving or pressure-piped scrolls, the skill lies in holding the piping bag correctly, working with the right consistency of royal icing, and having the confidence to work directly on the cake. In many of my master classes, I find students need a little encouragement and practice to build up their confidence. I therefore encourage them (and you) to practice these techniques on a plain iced board or an iced dummy cake. It is important to feel the viscosity of the icing, to know how much pressure to apply, and the correct speed at which to move the piping bag. To allow the icing to flow smoothly, always pull the piping bag in the same direction as the flow of icing.

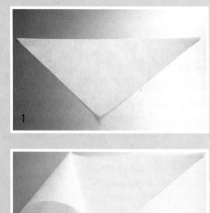

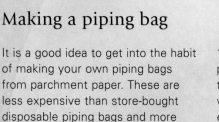

Making a piping bag

It is a good idea to get into the habit of making your own piping bags from parchment paper. These are less expensive than store-bought disposable piping bags and more hygienic than reusable piping bags.

1 Take a large sheet of parchment paper and divide it into equilateral triangles by folding and trimming with a small sharp knife, to use the entire sheet of paper. You can make piping bags of different sizes, which will be useful for different piping tasks. Start with one triangle in front of you—long side away from you and the opposite point facing you.

2 Bring the back of the left-hand point of the triangle down to meet the center point.

3 Lift the piping bag up, holding the 2 points that now meet in the center. Bring the right-hand point over the front of the bag all the way around to the back to meet the 2 points, so they all line up together.

4 Gently tease the base of the piping bag until the points line up and the bag is nice and taut and forms a sharp point at the tip of the bag.

5 Fold the base of the piping bag over on itself to seal, or staple twice.

Hand piping

1 Cut about ¾ inch off the point of a piping bag.

2 Drop an icing tip into the bag. Hold the bag in your hand like a cone, with the joint facing away from you. Spoon the royal icing into the bag as shown—no more than half full.

3 Press the front of the bag down so it is flush with the icing (this will begin to expel the air from the bag).

4 Fold the left-hand side of the bag inward, followed by the right-hand side, as shown.

5 Finally, fold and roll the top of the bag downward until it is secure. The piping bag is now ready to use.

6 Hand piping is a two-handed operation. Hold the piping bag in the hand you write with, between your first and second fingers. Use your thumb as the pressure pad on the back of the bag. Your thumb will apply all the pressure to force the icing out; the fingers merely hold the bag and direct the tip. Place the first finger of your other hand near the base of the tip to control its direction.

If you are piping on the sides of the cake, rest the base of both hands on the edge of the turntable, worktop, or (very lightly) the cake below. If you are piping on the top of the cake, rest the hand that is not holding the bag on the base, turntable, or worktop and have the piping hand rest on top of this one, so that at least one hand is in contact with a stable surface to steady the piping hand.

Make contact at the start and end of the piping, but lift the tip away from the cake and let the icing fall into position on the cake in between.

Hand-piped pearls and lines

Pearls are the most simple technique, yet they need to be executed cleanly to look professional and uniform. Pearls can be piped in a number of sizes, ranging from a delicate size no. 1 icing tip through 1.5, 2, and 3, to large pea-sized no. 4 pearls. The smaller the pearl, the easier it will be to disguise the peak that will inevitably form as you withdraw the tip. For larger pearls, this is harder to disguise, as the aperture is naturally that much larger, and peaks should be carefully dampened down with a moist paintbrush.

For perfect pearls, whether on the top, side, or base of the cake, hold the piping bag perpendicular to the cake and just a smidgen away from it. As you apply pressure, the icing comes into contact with the cake to create a perfect round base. Continue to apply pressure to allow the icing to build up to the desired size, then release the pressure and gently snatch the tip away at the same time and at the same angle to leave a perfect pearl (a).

Hand-piped lines
These tips can also be used to pipe vertical lines, from very fine (see Candy stripes, opposite) to chunky (b).

Line loops
Line loops are easily achieved with plain tips. Make contact at the start of the loop and again at the end, but pull the piping bag away from the cake as the loop is formed, to maintain a smooth loop (c).

Pearl loops
To build up confidence or additional texture, loops can be created by piping a trail of pearls that tail off before piping the next pearl, so they join up (d).

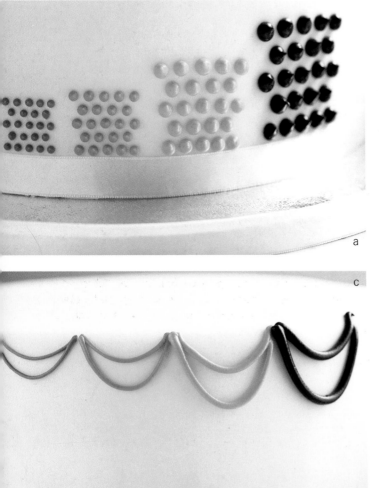

a

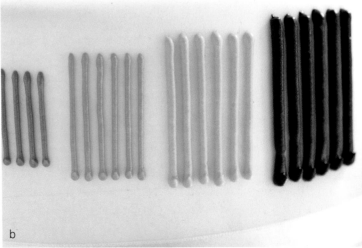

b

c

d

Candy stripes

Candy-striping cakes is a skillful technique that requires a steady hand and practice. It is effective for both individual and larger round cakes. Working with three colors of royal icing, this can be one of the most effective techniques to create a more masculine cake.

Add a few drops of water to the icing so that it is slightly slacker than usual, as this helps the icing to flow smoothly without breaking, helps the icing to adhere well to the cake, and reduces air bubbles. Fill three piping bags, each fitted with a no. 3 plain tip, with three different colors of icing, and seal the bags.

Place the piping bags in a sealable freezer bag and use one at a time to prevent the royal icing drying out in the bags.

For individual cakes, place the cakes on silver or gold cake cards prior to piping, so they can be handled once they have been decorated. Start the icing lines at the top of the cakes, as shown, and bring them right down to the base.

For large cakes, place an overturned cake board the same size as the cake on top of a covered cake and draw around the outside with a pokey tool. This will mark the top edge of the cake and be the guide from which you will always pipe down. This can be more time-consuming than the method for small cakes, but it is the only way to achieve accurate spacing.

TIP Remember to pinch the end of the tip each time you pick up a piping bag to ensure clean contact is made with the cake.

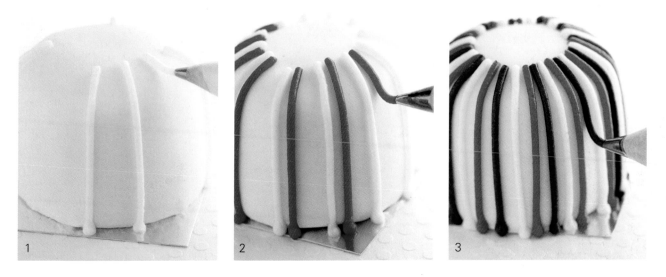

1 Place a cake in the center of a turntable and start with the white icing (if using), or else the palest color, and pipe a vertical line from the top edge to the base of the cake. Make contact at the top of the cake, then gently life the icing away from the cake as you move the piping bag downward. The icing should be coming out of the icing tip at right angles to the cake. Make contact at the base of the cake and allow the tip to build up a small pearl of royal icing before releasing the pressure and removing the tip. Repeat this around the cake 12 times to resemble a clock face, to set the spacing.

2 With the second color, pipe a vertical line parallel to the first color, ensuring you leave sufficient space for the third color. The lines should be parallel but not touching each other.

3 Apply the third color of candy stripes around the cake. Let set.

Scrolls and stars

Using a star icing tip, you can create single stars, textured piped lines, and scrolls. For single stars, hold the star tip at right angles to the cake and pipe as though for a pearl to create a star (a). To pipe a star trail—a trail of star pearls around the base of a cake (b)—use a no. 5 star tip.

1 For star scrolls, hold the icing tip against the top edge of the cake and begin to pipe to build up a star, pulling the piping bag below the star and to the right to tail off against the cake.

2 Pipe the next star scroll over the top of the end of the tail and bring the tail out of the top of the star toward the right, so creating a wave effect.

3 Continue working along the top of the cake in this manner until you finish the line of star scrolls.

Hand-piped bows

I pipe delicate bows using a no. 1.5 or no. 2 tip. Start in the center of the bow and pipe a triangle out to the top left, down to the bottom left, then back to the center. Touch the piping bag against the cake at these three points. Then move the piping bag out to the top right, down to the bottom right, then back to the center (a). Finish by piping the two tails from the center downward (b).

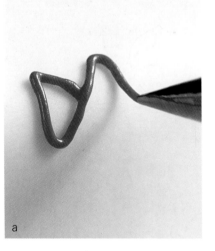

Hand-piped leaves

I just love the expression on the face of anyone who sees these royal iced leaves being piped without an icing tip or, indeed, has a go themselves. The royal icing is spooned into a piping bag with no tip. The technique relies on the decorator snipping the end of the piping bag evenly, and then pressure piping (see p. 94) to achieve these perfect leaves. The larger the snip, the bigger the leaf; the smaller the snip, the more delicate the leaf. What I particularly like is the fact that every leaf will be slightly different, making them so interesting. You could also use this technique with chocolate ganache.

Practice these leaves on a clean countertop or sheet of parchment paper until mastered; the icing can then be scraped up and spooned into a fresh piping bag. Alternatively, keep the ones you like and once they have dried overnight, peel them off with a small palette knife and ice them into position on your cake.

The most common areas people struggle with are not allowing the icing to build up before wiggling and moving the bag toward them, moving the bag too fast, and not releasing the pressure before pulling the leaf to a point.

  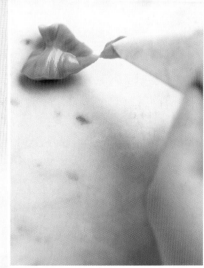

1 Fill a piping bag with green royal icing (add a little confectioners' sugar to ensure it is on the stiffer side) and seal the bag. Use a sharp pair of scissors to snip across the end of the piping bag at an angle, as shown and repeat the other way to create a V.

2 Hold the piping bag so the tip is flat, with the slits of the V to the sides, in contact with the cake. Apply pressure to the piping bag so the icing begins to build up. Gently lift the piping bag just off the cake and wiggle the bag gently from side to side using small smooth movements of your wrist, as you now gently pull the piping bag toward you.

3 Release the pressure on the bag, then pull the bag toward you and slightly upward to finish the leaf with a long tongue with a nice point.

Pressure piping

Our Little Venice lace design is hand piped using pressure piping. This is where the icing is built up on the cake and remains in contact with the cake rather than the tip being lifted and allowing the icing to fall into position. Depending on the design to be piped, a no. 2 or 3 tip is best to work with. The royal icing should be stiff but still glossy.

You will need:
royal icing

Equipment:
tracing paper and fine-tip pen
pokey tool
piping bag
no. 2 icing tip

1 Trace the template on p. 216, spacing the designs regularly around the cake. Fix the tracing paper to the cake and prick through the design with a pokey tool. Mark the center of all the pearls or beginning points of the scrolls with the pokey tool. Fit a piping bag with a no. 2 tip and fill with icing.

2 Pipe the 2 outer scrolls, bringing each inward and downward.

3 Pipe the highest 2 scrolls, which should come between the second-highest scroll and the pearl above.

4 Pipe the second line of scrolls up to and just on the first scroll line.

5 Pipe the third scrolls down; these are a little thicker, which is achieved by applying a little more pressure.

6 Pipe the first 2 vertical scrolls.

7 Pipe the smaller 2 vertical scrolls beneath the first.

8 Pipe the 2 outer pearls along the top edge.

9 Pipe the 2 base pearls of the top, which are slightly more elongated.

10 Pipe 2 rounder pearls above and finish with one elongated pearl at the very top of the design.

TIPS Start symmetrical designs at the top and work downward. Bring the left and right scrolls together to the center line. First pipe the left- and then immediately the right-hand mirror image of each separate scroll before moving on to the next mirrored pair.

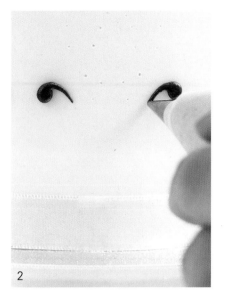

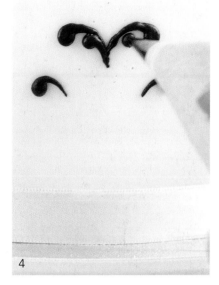

Basket weave

This technique never fails to impress. Two piping bags are used: one to create the vertical straight line and the other for the horizontal woven effect. The skill is keeping all the lines even and straight.

1 Place an overturned cake board the same size as the cake on top of a covered cake and draw around the outside with a pokey tool. This will mark the top edge of the cake and be the guide from which you will always pipe down.

2 Fill 2 piping bags—one fitted with a no. 3 plain tip, the other with a no. 19B basket-weave grooved tip—with white royal icing, and seal the bags. Starting with the plain tip, pipe a vertical line from the top edge to the base.

3 Now change to the basket-weave tip and hold it flat against the cake to the left of the piped line. Make contact with the cake as you begin to pipe, lifting the bag slightly away from the cake to create a gentle wave back on itself, and then bring the tip across the line horizontally and straight, tailing the icing away. The basket piping should be approximately 5/8-inch long.

4 Leave a gap the same width as the basket piping, then repeat the piping directly below the first line, and then all the way to the base of the cake—always leaving a gap (a).

5 Pipe the next vertical line approximately 3/8 inch away from, and parallel to, the first line, covering the tails of the basket piping (b).

6 Pipe the first row of the next section of basket piping between the first and second rows of the first section, so the icing starts at the first vertical line, pipes over the second vertical line, then tails away.

7 Repeat this technique all the way around the cake, keeping the pressure even all the way around, so the basket weave doesn't end up with gaps or is uneven.

TIPS Don't underestimate how much royal icing you will require for the basket piping—you will need several bags to decorate one tier.

Always start at the back of the cake in case the piping doesn't line up when you get all the way around. The front of the cake can then be positioned on show.

You will need:
white royal icing

Equipment:
cake board
pokey tool
2 piping bags
no. 3 icing tip
no. 19B basket-weave
    grooved icing tip

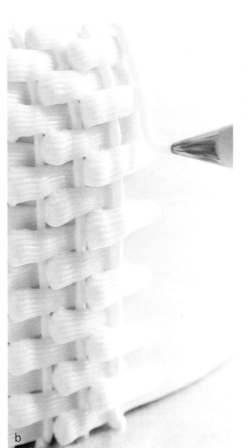

a

b

Run-outs

Piped outlines can be filled with icing to create effective decorations, such as the butterflies shown here. Diluting the icing to flooding consistency enables it to run out into the areas within the iced lines.

You will need:
royal icing in 2 colors: white for the outlines and bodies and a colored flooding icing (see p. 79) for the wings

Equipment:
tracing paper and fine-tip pen
cake board
masking tape
waxed paper
piping bags
no. 1.5 icing tip
paintbrush

1 To make the butterflies, trace the template on p. 214 enough times for all the butterflies you want, and fix the tracing paper onto a cake board with masking tape. Fix a sheet of waxed paper over the top with masking tape. Fit a piping bag with the icing tip and fill with some of the white royal icing. Pipe the outline of the wings.

2 Fill a piping bag with the colored flooding icing and snip the very end of the bag off. Flood the top wings of each butterfly in turn.

3 Use the paintbrush to draw the icing up to the hand-piped line.

4 Pipe small pearls of white icing to form the butterflies' markings. Let set 20 minutes.

5 Flood the bottom wings of each butterfly in turn, and use the paintbrush as before.

6 Add each butterfly's markings. Let set 20 minutes.

To assemble, use the piping bag and tip to pipe a head and body for each butterfly on top of a cake. Gently peel the butterfly wings off the waxed paper with a small palette knife. Place one wing on either side of the body at an angle. Place a small square of sponge under each wing to prop it up (see p. 144). Let set at least 1 hour before removing the sponge squares.

The finished results are shown on the Baskets in Bloom cake on p. 146.

1

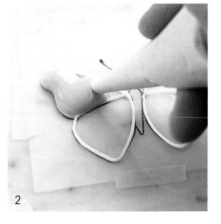

2

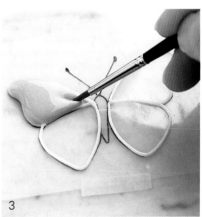

3

4

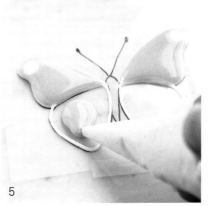

5

6

Hand molding

Hand-molded decorations can include just about anything, from flowers, animals, and insects to figurines, boats, and cars. These models are an effective decoration, requiring a set of professional tools and nimble fingers. The beauty is that the models can be made well in advance and lifted onto the covered cake, allowing the decorator to build up confidence. I have included hand-molded roses, bumble-bees, and ladybugs in this master class section, as they can be used on so many cake designs—from cupcakes to crown cakes, single-tier party cakes to fully tiered wedding cakes. You will find more specific projects using hand molding in the Cake Gallery section.

You can use rolled fondant to make the hand-molded roses in this section, but for finer-detailed or much larger models, use petal paste (also known as modeling paste). This is similar to rolled fondant, with the addition of gum tragacanth, which allows the paste to be rolled or handled in a much thinner and finer form than usual, and sets really firm very quickly. Petal paste can be bought from specialist cake decorating stores. Alternatively, add 1 tsp. gum tragacanth powder to 3½ oz. rolled fondant and knead well.

The paste will need to be kept in a sealed freezer bag when not being used, to prevent it from drying out. Use shortening, such as Crisco, on your fingertips if the paste is a little dry or crumbly.

Invest in a set of modeling tools—these include a ball tool, markers, a smiley tool, a pokey tool, a foam pad, a friller, some sugar glue, paintbrushes, and scissors.

For light dusting, make a small dusting bag using a square of cheesecloth filled with a mixture of confectioners' sugar combined with cornstarch, tied with a rubber band.

Hand-molded rose

Once mastered, this method of making a hand-molded rose is quick and easy, and you should be able to make a rose in less than 1 minute! The method here refers only to making rolled fondant roses, but you can use the same method for making chocolate plastique or petal paste roses. Rolled fondant roses are perfect for crown cakes or larger cakes where they are actually going to be eaten. Chocolate plastique roses can be made in white, milk, or dark chocolate plastique. You could even try making the center petals with darker shades and use lighter shades on the outside. Petal paste roses are for more delicate decorations and, while more refined, will be too hard and brittle to consume. If making petal paste roses, use no more than 2 oz. at a time. See overleaf for the full process. For a spectacular finishing touch, these roses, which can be made in varying sizes, can all be sprayed and then dredged in edible glitter.

You will need:
rolled fondant, as follows:
for a 2½-inch diameter rose: 2 oz.
for a 1¼-inch diameter rose: 1 oz.
for a ¾-inch diameter rose: ½ oz.
confectioners' sugar, for dusting

Equipment:
knife
letter-size plastic document holder cut open on 3 sides with a pair of scissors or knife

On a clean countertop, knead the rolled fondant until pliable but not soft and warm. Work on a piece of paste weighing no more than 5½ oz. at a time, and keep the remainder in a sealed freezer bag to prevent it drying out. The paste should be gently tacky but not sticky. Use the confectioners' sugar to dust sparingly if the paste is particularly warm and sticking.

Use the whole flat of your hand to roll it into a sausage—the diameter should be ⅝ inch for a small rose, 1 inch for medium, and 1½ inches for large.

1 Trim the end with a sharp knife and set aside. Cut 6 disks per rose from the sausage—the thickness for each should be ⅛ inch, regardless of the size of the finished rose.

2 Open the plastic document holder and lay the 6 disks down with the straight edge facing you and the rounded edges facing away. Replace the cover of the pouch over the disks.

3 With the base of your thumb, gently and quickly press each disk just once to begin to flatten it slightly. (You will need to work fairly swiftly to prevent the paste from drying out and cracking.)

4 To thin the petals, start at the base side of each petal, smoothing your thumb around the curved edge of the petal in a smooth motion. Leave the flat base of each of the petals untouched.

5 Gently lift up the plastic and look for the smallest petal.

6 Using your thumb, gently rub the petal, starting from the thick, chunky base, to release it from the plastic.

7 As the petal comes away, turn it over so it naturally curls away from you, and lay it over your first finger. The thinner, rounded petal part should be facing away from you over your finger, while the thicker, chunky base rests this side of your finger, parallel to your finger.

8–9 Starting on one side of the petal, gently roll it, curling it up horizontally across your finger inward to form the center of the rose.

10 Rub the second petal off the plastic in the same way and lay it over your finger. Lay the seam or joint of the central rose in contact with the second petal, so that the top of the central rose is halfway down the second petal. (Do not be tempted to lay the central rose too high.)

11 Gently pinch the second petal around the base of the central rose. Use your finger gently to press and shape the outer edge of the second petal down.

12 Repeat with the third petal, laying the seam of the second petal in the center of the third petal, so the top of the rose is halfway down the third petal.

13 Pinch around the base and gently shape the petal.

14–17 The final 3 petals form the outer layer of the rose. Lay, pinch, and shape them in exactly the same way, so that each covers one third of the outer layer of the rose.

18 Use a sharp knife to slice the chunky base off the rose and set aside on a cake board to firm about 2 hours.

TO STORE The roses can be kept safely in an airtight container at room temperature up to 3 months.

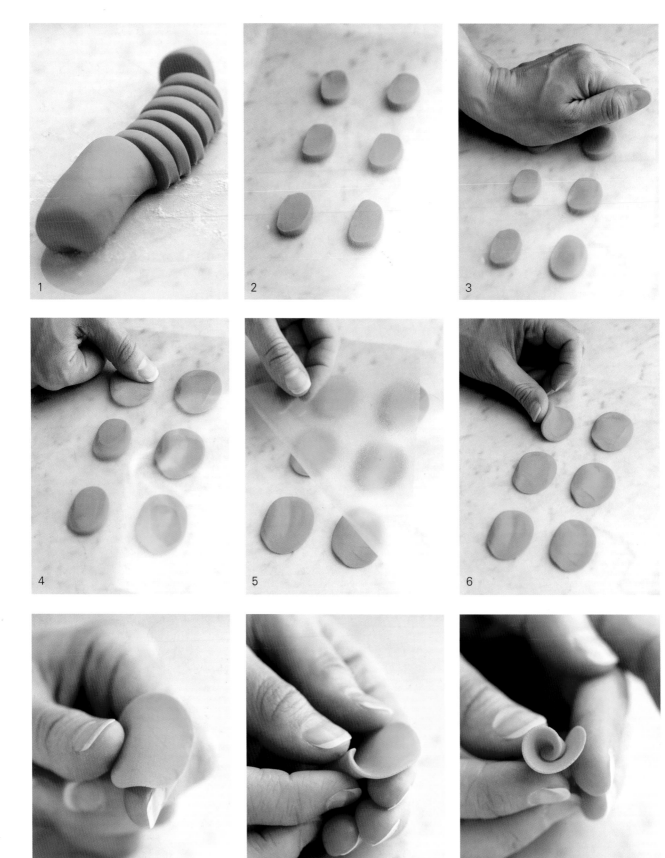

10

11

12

13

14

15

16

17

18

Bumblebee

These bumblebees are very cute. They can be made well in advance and used to add the finishing detail to a number of cakes.

Roll a hazelnut-size piece of yellow rolled fondant into a ball, and elongate slightly. Use the smiley tool to create a smile on one end. Roll out the white petal paste very finely and cut out 2 wings per bumblebee with the single petal cutter.

Paint 3 or 4 black stripes around the bumble bee's body, using the black color dust dissolved in some dipping alcohol. Pipe a small blob of white royal icing on the top of the bumblebee and fix both wings into position. Pipe 2 small white pearls for eyes and let set slightly before adding a smaller black pearl on each eye.

Let dry approximately 30 minutes.

You will need:
yellow rolled fondant (see p. 68)
white petal paste
½ tsp. black color dust
1 tsp. dipping alcohol
white royal icing
black royal icing (see
   pp. 77—8)

Equipment:
small rolling pin
smiley tool
³/₈-inch single petal cutter
paintbrush
piping bags
2 no. 1.5 icing tips

You will need:
red petal paste
black color dust
dipping alcohol
white royal icing

Equipment:
line-marking tool
paintbrush
piping bag
no. 1.5 icing tip

Ladybug

Like the bumblebees, these ladybugs are cute and can be used to dress individual cakes, larger cakes, or cupcakes.

Roll a small fingernail-sized piece of red petal paste into a ball and elongate slightly to one tapered end.

Use the line-marking tool to indent a line the length of the ladybug.

Dissolve some black color dust in some dipping alcohol, then paint 6 black spots on the ladybug's back.

Paint the blunter end black for the face.

Pipe 2 small white pearls for eyes. Let dry approximately 30 minutes.

Cutters

There are many cutters available, so it is worth building up your collection because you will need them. I have focused on cutters to create different flowers and leaves in this section. Some will cut out one petal at a time, some will cut out a number of petals, and others can cut petals and indent veins and other detail all at the same time. These flowers will be more refined, but I have chosen not to wire them, making them faster to create and safer to include on cakes.

Leaves

There are many leaf cutters available, but I like to use ones that indent the detail onto the leaf at the same time as cutting and pressing them out. They are available in various sizes.

1 Knead the green petal paste until smooth and pliable. Dust the counter top lightly with confectioners' sugar. Roll the petal paste out to a thickness of 1/8 inch. Place the leaf cutter on the paste and press the base to cut out the leaf.

2 Press the top of the cutter to indent the veining detail onto the leaf. Release.

3 Lift the cutter with the leaf still inside, then press the top again to push the leaf out of the cutter.

4 Hold the leaf and gently twist to create form and texture. Let dry and firm on some parchment paper 1 hour.

You will need:
green petal paste
confectioners' sugar,
 for dusting

Equipment:
small rolling pin
leaf plunger cutter
parchment paper

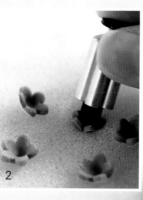

Plunger flowers

These blossoms are great as small filler flowers to add the finishing touch to christening cakes, crown cakes, and Easter garlands. They can be made from rolled fondant or petal paste in every color, with hand-piped centers in a contrasting color. Make these up well in advance and keep them stored in an airtight container.

1 Knead the lilac rolled fondant until smooth and pliable. Dust the worktop lightly with confectioners' sugar. Roll out the paste to a thickness of $1/8$ inch. Place the cutter on the paste and press the base to cut out the flower.

2 Lift the cutter away from the paste with the flower still intact. Place on the top of a clean sponge and press the top of the plunger to remove the flower and form the petals at the same time.

3 Let dry and firm on some parchment paper 1 hour. Fit the piping bag with the icing tip and fill with white royal icing. Ice a center in each flower.

You will need:
lilac rolled fondant (see p. 68)
confectioners' sugar, for dusting
1 recipe white royal icing (see p. 77)

Equipment:
small rolling pin
$1^{1}/_{2}$-inch plunger flower cutter
sponge
parchment paper
piping bag
no. 1.5 icing tip

Large open roses

Each layer of these petal-paste roses has to be molded and shaped with a ball tool. Although they are time consuming to make, the result is a delicate, refined open rose that will decorate the finest of cakes

You will need:
red petal paste
confectioners' sugar, for dusting
sugar glue
black royal icing (see pp. 77–78)

Equipment:
small rolling pin
5-petal cutters: 1¼, 1¾, and 2½ inches in diameter
foam pad
ball tool
aluminum foil
piping bag
no. 1.5 icing tip

1 Knead the red petal paste until smooth and pliable. Dust the worktop lightly with confectioners' sugar. Roll the petal paste out to a thickness of ⅛ inch. Cut out a small, medium, and large 5-petal rose shape.

2 Place each rose shape in turn on the foam pad. Use the ball tool to gently thin, shape, and form each petal on all the rose shapes.

3 Starting with the largest rose shape, place it on some crinkled aluminum foil to give the flower a sense of movement.

4 Brush a small amount of sugar glue in the center of the rose.

5 Fix the medium-size rose on top, giving it a turn so it sits between the larger petals.

6 Finally, add the smallest rose on top. Fit the piping bag with the icing tip and fill with black royal icing. Hand-pipe small black pearls into the center of the rose. Let the rose dry and firm on the foil 2 hours before using.

Poppies / Frilly roses

These open poppies can also be adapted for a frilly rose. Smaller than the open rose, they are delicate and quick to make. Add a piped center, glitter pearl, or painted detail to vary the flowers.

You will need:
red petal paste
confectioners' sugar, for dusting
sugar glue
black petal paste

Equipment:
small rolling pin
1½-inch 5-petal flower cutter
foam pad
ball tool
pokey tool
parchment paper

1 Knead the red petal paste until smooth and pliable. Dust the worktop lightly with confectioners' sugar. Roll out the petal paste to a thickness of ⅛ inch. Cut out 2 flowers with the cutter.

2 Place the flowers on the foam pad. Use a ball tool to thin the petal edges and shape the flowers.

3 Brush one of the flowers with sugar glue.

4 Position the second flower on top of the first, ensuring the petals sit between the petals on the base flower.

5 Roll a small pea-sized piece of black petal paste and flatten slightly. Fix in the center of the flower with sugar glue and use the pokey tool to indent over the surface.

6 Let the open poppy dry and firm 1 hour on some parchment paper before using.

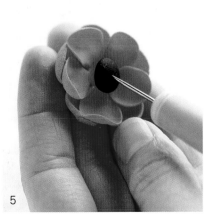

Daffodils

Daffodils are the perfect flowers to make for all your spring cakes. Their three-dimensional shape is impressive, adding texture to crown cakes and larger cakes alike.

1 Knead the yellow petal paste until smooth and pliable. Dust the worktop lightly with confectioners' sugar. Roll the paste out to a thickness of ⅛ inch. Cut out 2 petal layers and one trumpet shape with the daffodil cutter.

2 Place the pieces on the foam pad. Use the small ball tool to thin the petal edges and to thin and frill the longer curved edge of the daffodil trumpet.

3 Lift the daffodil trumpet and roll it up, with the frilled edge facing upward.

4 Fit the piping bag with the icing tip and fill with yellow royal icing. Fix the 2 petal layers together with some icing, ensuring the upper layer sits between the petals on the base layer. Pipe a pearl of icing in the center of the upper layer.

5 Fix the daffodil trumpet into position in the center of the daffodil. Let dry and firm on some parchment paper 1 hour.

You will need:
yellow petal paste
confectioners' sugar, for dusting
yellow royal icing (see pp. 77–78)

Equipment:
small rolling pin
1½-inch daffodil cutter
foam pad
small ball tool
piping bag
no. 1.5 icing tip
parchment paper

Buttercups

These cheerful petal-paste buttercups would look perfect on an Easter cake, cute crown cakes, or little girl's christening cake. They can be prepared well in advance and dusted with a little yellow glitter for added sparkle.

1 Assemble the yellow petal paste (which should be kneaded until smooth and pliable), the confectioners' sugar, and sugar glue, along with the equipment.

2 Dust the countertop lightly with confectioners' sugar. Roll the paste out to a thickness of 1/8 inch. Cut out a 5-petal shape and a plunger flower for each flower required and place on the foam pad. Use the ball tool to shape each petal gently so that they are nicely curved.

3 Brush the center of the 5-petal shape with some sugar glue and place the plunger flower centrally on top. Let dry and firm on some parchment paper 1 hour.

You will need:
yellow petal paste
confectioners' sugar, for dusting
sugar glue

Equipment:
small rolling pin
1-inch 5-petal flower cutter
3/8-inch plunger flower cutter
foam pad
ball tool
parchment paper

Ribbons

Ribbons can add dramatic effect to a cake and provide the finishing touch. Single satin ribbon (shiny on one side) is perfect for edging base boards. Double satin (shiny on both sides) is ideal for surrounding the base of cakes and for ribbon bows, ribbon insertion, and wired ribbon loops. Grosgrain (a ribbed matte finish) works well with chocolate-covered cakes but is not suitable for ribbon loops. Organza (sheer and transparent) adds a delicate touch between flowers or tied around the center of cakes. It should not be used to edge base boards or to seal around the base edge of a cake. It is perfect for wired ribbon loops.

Ribbon bows

You will need:
ribbon

Equipment:
small, sharp scissors

Double satin ribbons give the best results for these ribbon bows.

1 Make a loop at the end of a length of ribbon so the shorter tail is positioned away from you and held between your thumb and first or second finger. This will become the right-hand loop of the finished ribbon bow.

2 Bring the long tail over your thumb and around the back of the loop with your other hand. The loop over the thumb will become the center tie holding the bow together.

3 Push the back of the long tail through the center tie that is resting over your thumb.

4 As the ribbon comes through the center tie, it will form the left-hand loop of the ribbon bow.

5 Hold the left-hand loop and tail in your left hand and the right-hand loop and tail in your right hand, and pull taut to form a neat bow.

6 Hold the center tie and pull each tail to make the loops smaller, neater, and even.

7 Trim the tails to the desired length.

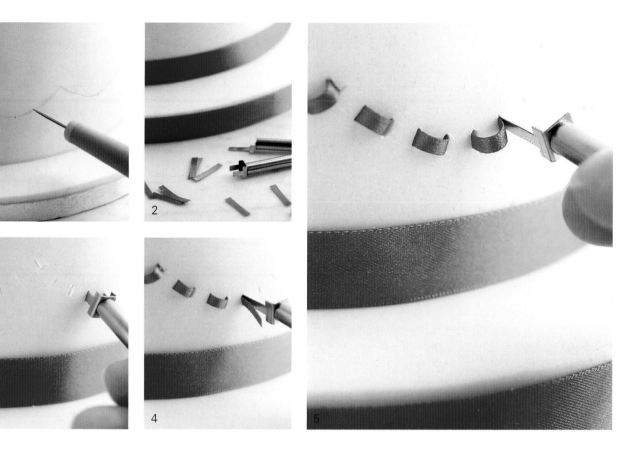

Ribbon insertion

Ribbon insertion is a clever technique to create the illusion that a ribbon has been threaded through the rolled fondant coat on a cake. A special ribbon insertion tool has two blades, which will be used as a pair: a slit-making tool to create the icing slits and an insertion blade to tuck the ribbon in gently on both sides. Work with double satin ribbon in a solid contrasting color for best effect. Top the ribbon insertion loops with handmade bows made from the same ribbon, if desired.

1 Trace the template of the desired design and transfer it onto the cake using the pokey tool.

2 Cut a length of ribbon into little strips each approximately ⅝ inch in length.

3 Following the marked design, insert the slit-making tool through the layer of rolled fondant, then remove it. Place the left side of the marker tool in the right-hand slit just created to make sure you keep the spacing even as you work around the cake.

4 To insert the ribbon, hold a cut strip of ribbon in your left hand with one edge of the ribbon held at the left slit. Use the insertion tool to push the ribbon into the precut slit until it is secured.

5 Direct the other end of the ribbon to the adjoining slit and use the insertion tool to push this edge securely into the precut slit. Repeat all the way around the cake.

TIPS Cut the ribbon strips as evenly as possible when preparing them.

Ensure the loops are even either by pushing the ribbon in more firmly if a loop looks too loose, or gently pulling a loop out if it is too taut.

If you are making ribbon bows to match the insertion, make these first, so that you can snip the discarded tail cut-offs into strips to be used for insertion.

Ribbon loops (wired)

You will need:
ribbon
28-gauge white wires cut into
6 inch lengths
white floral tape

Equipment:
small, sharp scissors

Wired ribbon loops can be used to complete a floral display, as they will fill gaps between more fragile, brittle sugar flowers. Use a combination of double satin and organza ribbons in different widths and colors to give your cakes maximum impact.

1 Make a loop approximately 4 inches high at the end of a length of ribbon, so the shorter tail is positioned away from you and held between your thumb and first finger.

2 Fold the longer length of ribbon back on itself to create a second loop the same size as the first.

3 Repeat this step to create a third ribbon loop.

4 Fold the ribbon back again as if to start a fourth loop, but cut the ribbon as a single length only, to create a 4-inch tail.

5 Place a length of wire behind and at the base of the ribbon loops, with approximately ¾ inch of wire protruding.

6 Fold this shorter length of wire back on itself.

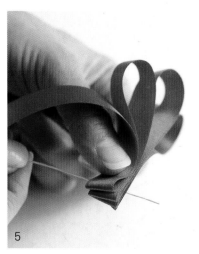

7 Twist the shorter end tightly around the longer length of wire.

8 Bend the twisted wire down so the ribbon loop becomes the top.

9 Pass a length of white floral tape behind the twisted wire.

10 Pull the tape taut to cover the ribbon twist and the base of the ribbon loops together.

11 Seal the tape against the wire approximately 2 inches down.

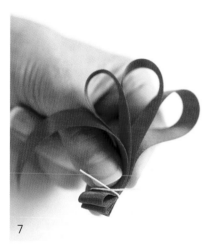

7

8

9

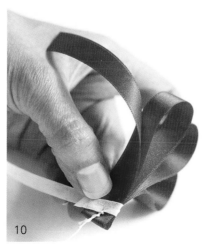

10

11

Hand painting

Hand painting onto cakes covered with rolled fondant can be a wonderful way of creating a really individual cake, as no two will ever be the same. For me, this process combines two passions: cake decorating and painting. Our students create wonderful designs when we hold hand painting master classes, as the technique is less foreign to them than piping—they are more comfortable and confident handling a paintbrush than a piping bag.

Take inspiration from nature, textiles, and books to design the initial concept. Build up the layers of paint using melted cocoa butter and color dusts to create an oil-painting effect, which sits on the surface of the cake. Hand painting can be free-flowing, as you add and blend colors, finishing the design with precision detail where necessary.

Cocoa butter, which comes in buttons, is available from specialist cake decorating stores and online. It keeps 12 months in an airtight container. Color dusts come in a wide spectrum of colors—usually in bottles or jars. It is essential to include white and black.

Invest in a collection of paintbrushes: larger heads for building up the base color, and an assortment, varying from medium to fine heads, for adding precision detail.

Place a few buttons of cocoa butter on a saucer suspended over a bowl of boiling water. Position little piles of color dust on the edge of the saucer, around the melted cocoa butter. Blend each color (and mixtures of colors) with the cocoa butter to achieve the colors you require. The results provide a translucent color when painted onto rolled fondant. Adding white color dust to the mix will strengthen the color, so it is bolder.

Reversing the concept can be a nice idea, so coloring the rolled fondant used to cover your cake, then painting the design detail in white, which will really stand out well (see the Passion Flower cake on p. 198).

If you make a mistake, you can use an absorbent cloth to soak off the paint—or simply wait for it to dry and then paint over it.

Hand painting using color dusts blended with dipping alcohol can be used to add detail to hand-molded or cut-out flowers, insects, and models. The painted detail dries much faster, soaking into the icing to create added interest (see the Summer Butterflies cake on p. 144).

Hand painting clear edible gel or metallic lusters onto pearls and scrolls or chocolate flowers adds the finishing touch for a truly professional cake. (see the Purlesque cake on p. 120).

You will need:
color dusts in red, burgundy
  black, and white

Equipment:
tracing paper and fine-tip pen
pokey tool
nontoxic pencil (optional)
paintbrushes in various sizes

1 Trace the design on p. 214 using the fine-tip pen, and transfer it onto the cake using the pokey tool. Alternatively, lightly sketch the roses on the cake with the nontoxic pencil.

2 Beginning with the largest paintbrush and the red color dust, paint the background of each rose onto the cake.

3 Let set briefly, then start again from the beginning, changing brushes as you build up layers of more red and darker burgundy with soft, circular, sweeping brush strokes.

4 Using another brush, blend the black paint with the red, then add a center to each rose and more brush strokes on the petals.

5 Finish by highlighting each rose with a swirl of white brush strokes, using the finest brush.

6 Let the painting dry.

Cake Gallery

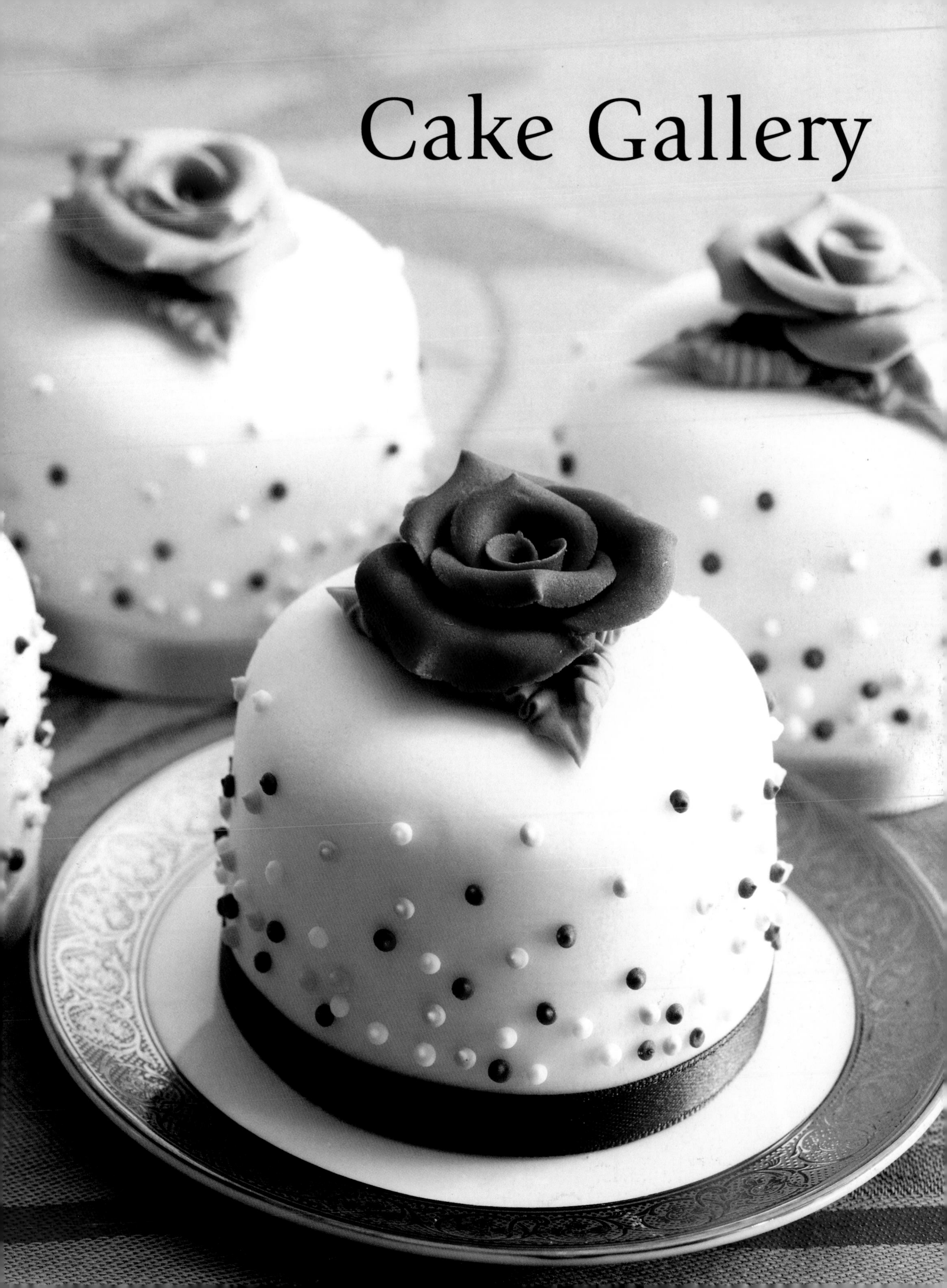

Welcome to the Cake Gallery. The collection of cakes in this section will feature techniques I have covered in the Master Class, with additional skills specific to each design. Whether you want to create a selection of beautiful afternoon tea cakes, a fun birthday cake, or a stunning four-tier wedding cake adorned with flowers and painted couture roses, my intention has been to give you a number of designs aimed at putting all your new skills into practice. Many of these designs are interchangeable, and I would encourage you to experiment to create your own cakes using these designs as inspiration.

Purlesque

I love the simplicity of this cake—but you shouldn't underestimate just how long it takes to decorate. No two pearls are touching, apart from the ring around the base of each tier. The inspiration came from a clustered Chanel pearl necklace. It is a wonderful challenge for the beginner and more accomplished cake decorator alike to perfect their pearls.

a

b

Preparing the cake

Place the cakes on the cake boards of the same size and cover with a base coat of your choice, as shown on p. 71 and the ivory rolled fondant top coat, as shown on p. 72. Line the base board with ivory rolled fondant, as shown on p. 73, and surround with the ivory ribbon, fixed with glue. Leave the cakes and base board to dry overnight.

Fix the base tier centrally into position on the base board with royal icing. Dowel and direct stack the tiers, using 6 dowels per tier, as shown on p. 83. Place the cake on a turntable.

You will need:

4-inch, 6-inch, 8-inch, and 10-inch round cakes

4-inch, 6-inch, 8-inch, and 10-inch thick round cake boards

marzipan, rolled fondant, or white chocolate plastique, for the base coat (see pp. 71 and 72 for quantities)

ivory rolled fondant (see p. 68), for the top coat (see p. 72 for quantities)

14-inch round base board

ivory rolled fondant, for the base board (see p. 72 for quantity)

3 feet 9 inches ivory ribbon, ⅝ inch wide

18 doweling rods

2 recipes royal icing, divided between 3 bowls and one colored ivory, one caramel, and one left white (see pp. 76–78)

clear edible gel

topaz and gold lusters

dipping alcohol

Equipment:

small, sharp scissors

glue stick

turntable

6 piping bags

2 no. 1.5 , 2 no. 2, and 2 no. 3 icing tips

paintbrush

Decorating the cake

1 Fit the piping bags with the different sized tips and fill with the royal icings as follows: caramel: large and small; white: large and medium; ivory: medium and small. Pipe a row of pearls around the base of each tier to seal the cake. Now place all the bags in a sealed freezer bag while you use the no. 3 tip with white.

2 Starting with the top tier, pipe perfect, large, random white pearls over the tier and down the sides. Use a paintbrush to remove any peaks as necessary—although once the cake is fully encrusted with pearls and they have been glazed, these are unlikely to be as noticeable.

3 Move onto the next piping bag, with a different color, and add extra pearls over the top and sides of the cake, making sure they do not directly touch any of the white pearls.

4 Continue building up the design with more pearls in different shades and different sizes until the cake is fully encrusted (a). I chose to peter out the pearls slightly as I worked my way down the cake, but you may prefer not to.

5 Brush the white pearls with clear edible gel. Mix some topaz luster with dipping alcohol and brush a selection of the ivory pearls with topaz luster. Next, mix some topaz and gold luster together with some more dipping alcohol and brush this over a selection of the caramel pearls (b).

Art Nouveau

The Art Nouveau era at the start of the twentieth century, with its fluid, floaty, and asymmetrical style, was the precursor to the Art Deco era of symmetry and angular graphic designs. This delicate cake, highlighting swirls and pearls, and with a simple blossom on the top, would be perfect for a baby shower, christening, or birthday cake.

Preparing the cake

Place the cakes on the cake boards of the same size and cover with a base coat of your choice, as shown on p. 71, and the white rolled fondant top coat, as shown on p. 72. Surround the cake with the 1-inch ribbon and fix with a dab of royal icing. Cover the base board with white rolled fondant, as shown on p. 73. Surround the board with the 5/8-inch pink ribbon, fixed into position with glue. Leave the cake and the base board to dry overnight. Place the cake on the lined base board.

You will need:

4-inch round cake

4-inch thick round cake board

marzipan, rolled fondant, or white chocolate plastique, for the base coat (see pp. 71 or 72 for quantity)

white rolled fondant, for the top coat (see p. 72 for quantity)

14 inches pink ribbon, 1 inch wide

6-inch round base board

white rolled fondant, for the base board (see p. 72 for quantity)

22 inches pink ribbon, 5/8 inch wide

1 recipe royal icing, divided into 2 bowls and 1 colored pale pink and 1 green (see pp. 76–78)

white open petal paste poppy-style flower with a hand-piped pink center (see p. 107)

Equipment:

glue stick

tracing paper and fine-tip pen

pokey tool

2 piping bags

no. 1.5 icing tip

Decorating the cake
1 Trace the design on p. 219 and transfer it onto the top and sides of the cake, using the pokey tool.

2 Fit a piping bag with the icing tip and fill with pink icing. Pipe a fine trail, allowing the icing to fall into position on the cake.

3 Build up a delicate row of pearls along the top edge of the hand-piped line.

4 Repeat, but this time add the pearls along the underside edge of the line.

5 Pipe the next line using the same-size tip and piping bag to build up the design, covering the indent created by the pokey tool.

6 Finish with a single row of pearls around the cake directly above the ribbon.

7 Fill the second piping bag with the green royal icing, snip the end as shown on p. 93 and pipe 3 green leaves in the center. Place the white poppy-style flower on the leaves and leave to set overnight.

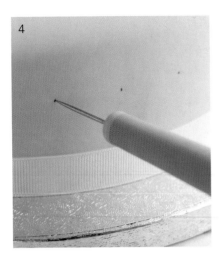

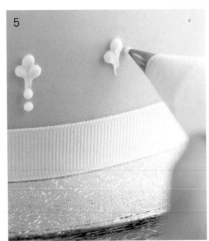

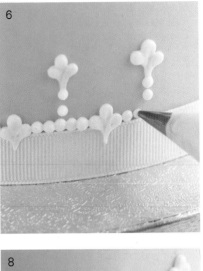

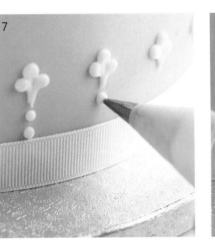

4 On the second tier (pink), use a ruler and pokey tool to mark every 1¼ inches, ⅝ inch above the ribbon, where each of the fleur-de-lys designs will be piped.

5 Pipe the design using the no. 2 tip, with 2 pearls below.

6 Pipe a fleur-de-lys design between the first row, sitting directly on the ribbon. Join these fleurs-de-lys with a chain of pearls piped with the no. 2 tip.

7 Repeat the design from the first (white) tier onto the third (white) tier. Then repeat the design from the second (pink) tier onto the base (pink) tier.

8 Concentrate on just piping a fleur-de-lys design on the base-tier ribbon, omitting the chain of pearls. Let dry overnight.

Dressing the cake

9 Surround the Styrofoam block with the 1-inch pink ribbon and fix with glue. To assemble, place the Styrofoam block on the base tier, fixed with some royal icing, and fix the 3 stacked tiers in position on top.

10 Roll 7 oz. of the remaining white rolled fondant into a ring. Dampen the top of the base tier ¾ inch inside the cake with a moistened paintbrush and fix the ring into position as shown on p. 201.

11 Fill a piping bag with pink royal icing and pipe a blob on the white rolled fondant ring. Fix the first open rose into position at an angle to bridge the gap between the third and base tiers. Fix a thin pink ribbon loop next to the open rose by pushing it into the rolled fondant ring.

12 Add a thicker pink ribbon loop and then a white organza ribbon loop in a similar way to fill the space, then butt the next open rose up against them, fixed into position with royal icing. Continue to work around the tier until full.

13 Use the remaining 2 oz. pink rolled fondant to create a dome for the top tier and fix into position with a little water. Push 3 pink ribbon loops into a triangular position in the dome and fix 3 pink glitter open roses between the loops with royal icing. Build up the top decoration with the remaining ribbon loops. Use the sharp scissors to snip the ribbon loop tails at a nice angle to complete the decoration.

Hello, Dolly!

I was inspired by the classic film *Hello, Dolly!* to design this majestic wedding cake. As Mrs. Dolly Levi makes her entrance to the Harmonia Gardens, she stands silently, with awesome presence, at the top of the sweeping red staircase wearing a gorgeous gold brocade and sequin dress, and her auburn hair is finished with yellow ocher and sage green feathers. This stunning cake commands the same center of attention, deserving its place as the focal point at the finest of weddings.

Preparing the cake

Place the cakes on cake boards of the same size and cover with a base coat of your choice, as shown on p .71, and the gold rolled fondant top coat, as shown on p. 72. Brush some gold luster over the cakes (a).

Line the base boards with gold rolled fondant, as shown on p. 73, then brush with gold luster. Surround the base boards with the ⅝-inch gold ribbon and fix with the glue stick. Leave the cakes and boards to dry overnight.

Decorating the cake

1 Trace the Hello, Dolly! template on p. 218 and transfer it onto each tier with the pokey tool, starting from the top and working downward (b).

2 Fix the base tier centrally into position on the smaller base board with a dab of royal icing, then fix the smaller base board to the larger one. Prepare the base tier to be blocked, as shown on p. 82, using 8 dowels. Surround all the tiers with the 1-inch gold ribbon, fixed into position with royal icing. Use the remaining 12 inches of ribbon to surround the Styrofoam block and fix with glue.

You will need:

4-inch, 6-inch, 8-inch, and 10-inch round cakes

4-inch, 6-inch, 8-inch, and 10-inch thick round cake boards

marzipan, rolled fondant, or white chocolate plastique, for the base coat (see pp. 71 and 72 for quantities)

gold rolled fondant (see p. 68), for the top coat (see p. 72 for quantities) and the base boards (see p. 73 for quantities), plus an extra 9 oz. for the ring and dome

gold luster

13-inch and 16-inch round base boards

8 feet gold ribbon, ⅝ inch wide

2 recipes gold royal icing (see pp. 76–78)

20 doweling rods

10 feet gold ribbon, 1 inch wide

6-inch round Styrofoam block, 2 inches deep

dipping alcohol

18 open roses (see p. 106), made with gold petal paste and finished with sage-green pearl centers

triple ribbon loops with tails (see pp. 112–113), as follows:

10 sage-green loops using 26 feet ribbon, ⅝ inch wide

10 rust-orange organza loops using 26 feet ribbon, ⅜ inch wide

10 red organza loops using 26 feet ribbon, 1 inch wide

Equipment:

paintbrush

small, sharp scissors

glue stick

tracing paper and fine-tip pen

pokey tool

piping bag

no. 3 icing tip

turntable

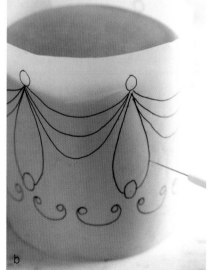

c

d

3 Fit a piping bag with the icing tip and fill with gold royal icing. Place the top tier onto a turntable and pipe the design as shown (c) (d). Repeat on the second and third tiers. Once all 3 tiers are finished, hand pipe the base tier in the same way. Set aside and allow all the tiers to dry overnight. Mix some gold luster with dipping alcohol at a ratio of 1:2 and paint all the hand-piped detail using the paintbrush.

4 To assemble, dowel and stack the top 3 tiers as shown on p. 83, using 6 dowels per tier. Add some royal icing to the top of the Styrofoam block on the base tier, then fix the 3 stacked tiers in place on top of it.

Dressing the cake

5 Roll 7 oz. of the remaining gold rolled fondant into a ring, dampen the top of the base tier ³⁄₄ inch inside the cake with a moistened paintbrush, and fix the rolled fondant ring into position (see p.147). Use the final 2 oz. of gold rolled fondant to create a dome for the top tier and fix into position with a little water.

6 Pipe a blob of icing on the rolled fondant ring. Fix the first open rose into position at an angle to bridge the gap between the third and base tiers.

7 Fix the first ribbon loop next to the open rose by pushing it into the rolled fondant ring. Add more ribbon loops in a similar way to fill the space, then butt the next open rose up against the ribbons, fixing it into position with royal icing. Continue to work around the space between the tiers until it is filled and there are no gaps (e).

8 For the top tier, push 3 ribbon loops into a triangular position in the gold rolled fondant dome and fix 3 gold open roses between the loops with royal icing. Build up the top decoration with the remaining loops. Snip the ribbon loop tails at a nice angle to complete the decoration.

Liberty Flowers

This design was created specifically for the renowned department store Liberty of London, taking inspiration from their neon colors and striking decorations. This design works well with a choice of two colors piped one way and in reverse. We have included fuchsia pink and lime here, but tangerine and fuchsia, navy and aqua, or caramel and ivory could all be very effective.

Preparing the cakes

Cover each cake with a base coat of your choice and the white rolled fondant top coat, as shown on p. 69. Let dry overnight. Surround half the cakes with pink ribbon and the other half with green ribbon, and fix into position with a dab of royal icing.

You will need (per cake):

2-inch individual round cake (see p. 69 for cutting instructions)

2½ oz. marzipan, rolled fondant, or white chocolate plastique, for the base coat

3 oz. white rolled fondant, for the top coat

8 inches pink or green ribbon, ⅝ inch wide

Plus:

1 recipe white royal icing, split into 2 bowls, one colored fuchsia, the other lime green (see pp.76–78)

Equipment:

small, sharp scissors
turntable
pokey tool
4 piping bags
2 no. 1.5 and no. 2 icing tips

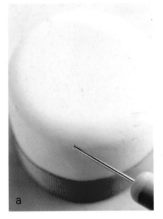

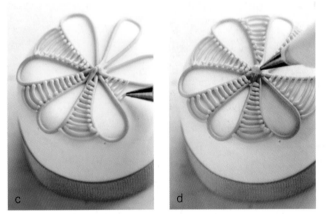

Decorating the cakes

1 Place a pink-ribboned cake on a turntable. Use the pokey tool to mark the center of each cake and the 6 points around the top of the cake where the petals will end (a).

2 Fit a piping bag with a no. 2 tip and fill with half the fuchsia pink royal icing. Starting at the center of the cake, pipe the first loop to the edge of the cake and back to the center (b). Turn the cake around and pipe the second loop directly opposite the first. Turn the cake and pipe 2 loops between the first and second, then spin the cake around and pipe the final 2 loops between the first and second on the opposite side, so you end up with 6 loops in total.

3 Fit another piping bag with a no. 1.5 tip and fill with half the lime green royal icing. Pipe small lines of green icing between each pink loop to the edge of the cake (c).

4 Finish by piping a pearl of green icing in the center of the decoration (d).

5 Decorate all the pink-ribboned cakes in this way, then switch the colors around and pipe the green-ribboned cakes with thicker green loops and thinner pink lines and central pearl, using the other 2 piping bags and icing tips.

Purple Azalea Lace

This cake has been surrounded with deep purple ribbon, decorated with our hand-piped Little Venice Cake Company lace design, and finished with rows of open azaleas with hand-piped pearls. This contemporary wedding cake combines pressure piping in a bold purple color, with the azalea-style roses. Less forgiving than hand piping in white, this technique will certainly test your skills. I have chosen to use a wide ribbon around the base of each tier to frame the azaleas and to still allow the piping to be fully appreciated. To make the tiers super deep, with an overall height of 4 inches, each cake is placed on a 1-inch deep Styrofoam dummy of the same size as the cake before covering.

You will need:

6-inch, 8-inch, and 10-inch round cakes

6-inch, 8-inch, and 10-inch round Styrofoam dummies, 1 inch deep

marzipan, rolled fondant, or white chocolate plastique, for the base coat (see pp. 71 and 72 for quantities)

white rolled fondant, for the top coat (see p. 72 for quantities)

13-inch and 16-inch round base boards

purple rolled fondant (see p. 68), for the base boards (see p. 72 for quantities)

7 feet 6 inches purple ribbon, 1½ inches wide

8 feet 3 inches purple ribbon, ⅝ inch wide

1 recipe purple royal icing (see pp.76–78)

12 doweling rods

45 white azalea-style roses (see the poppy method on p. 107)

3 fabric azaleas

Equipment:

small, sharp scissors
tracing paper and fine-tip pen
turntable
pokey tool
2 piping bags
no. 1.5 and no. 2 icing tips

Preparing the cake

Place each cake on a same-size Styrofoam dummy and cover both the cake and dummy together with a base coat of your choice, as shown on p. 71, and the white rolled fondant top coat, as shown on p. 72. Line the base boards with purple rolled fondant, as shown on p. 73. Surround all the tiers with 1½-inch purple ribbon, fixed into position with a dab of royal icing, and the base boards with ⅝-inch purple ribbon, fixed with glue. Let dry overnight.

Decorating the cake

1 Trace the LVCC Lace design on p. 216 and transfer onto the cakes with the pokey tool as a single row around the base of each tier directly above the ribbon. Place the top tier on a turntable.

2 Fit 1 of the piping bags with the no. 2 tip and fill with half the purple royal icing. Pressure-pipe the LVCC lace design (see pp. 94–95) around the top tier, before moving on to the middle then base tiers (a). Let dry overnight.

3 Fit the second piping bag with the no. 1.5 tip and fill with the remaining purple royal icing, then pipe pearls in the center of each of the azalea-style roses (b). Let dry overnight. Dowel and direct stack the top 3 tiers, using 6 dowels per tier, as shown on p. 83. Surround each tier with the roses, iced directly onto the deep purple ribbon. Finally, lay the fabric azaleas on the top.

Pompadour

I have used a subtle palette of pastel colors for this Pompadour cake and the individual versions overleaf. Delicately colored and decorated, with a lustered hand-piped design, this chic French-style cake would be lovely for a special dinner party celebration or anniversary.

Preparing the cake

Place the cake on the cake board and cover with a base coat of your choice, as shown on p. 71, and the pale pink rolled fondant top coat, as shown on p. 72. Surround the cake with the 1-inch ivory ribbon, fixed with a dab of royal icing. Line the base board with the pistachio green rolled fondant, as shown on p. 73, and surround it with the 5/8-inch ivory ribbon, fixed with glue. Leave the cake and board to dry overnight.

You will need:

6-inch square cake

6-inch thick square cake board

marzipan, rolled fondant, or white chocolate plastique, for the base coat (see pp. 71 and 72 for quantity)

pale pink rolled fondant (see p. 68), for the top coat (see p. 72 for quantity)

28 inches ivory grosgrain ribbon, 1 inch wide

1 recipe ivory royal icing (see pp. 76–78)

9-inch square base board

pistachio green rolled fondant (see p. 68), for the base board (see p. 72 for quantity)

38 inches ivory grosgrain ribbon, 5/8 inch wide

topaz luster

dipping alcohol

single fresh or sugar rose

Equipment:

small, sharp scissors

glue stick

tracing paper cut to the height of the cake and the length of one side

ruler

pokey tool

piping bag

no. 1.5 icing tip

paintbrush

Decorating the cake

1 Fix the cake centrally into position on the base board with royal icing. Hold the sheet of tracing paper in line with the top edge of the cake and mark 1-inch intervals with the pokey tool all around the cake.

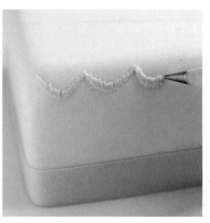

2 Fit the piping bag with the icing tip and fill with ivory royal icing. Hold the piping bag at the first point and wiggle your hand up and down to create a scalloped swag to the next marked point. Repeat the design around the cake, keeping the swags even in size.

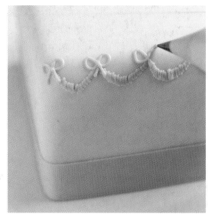

3 Pipe the bows at the top of each swag (see p. 92), starting at the center and allowing the line to come out to top right, straight down, then back to the center, before heading out to top left, straight down, then back to the center. Pipe the 2 ribbon bow tails. Repeat all the way around.

4 Pipe a vertical row of pearls straight down beneath the ribbon bows, with a larger pearl at the base.

5 Underneath the middle of each swag, pipe a triangle of 3, 2, 1 tiny pearls, as shown. Let set.

6 Blend some topaz luster and some dipping alcohol on a 1:2 ratio; brush over the entire design. Add the rose.

Pompadour Trinkets

The looped design used for the large Pompadour cake (see p. 136) transposes well onto these individual trinket cakes. The same design has been piped around the edge of the cakes, with a hand-painted ribbon bow added in the center. I have used shades of delicate colors that combine so well together.

You will need (per cake):

1½-inch individual square cake (see p. 66 for cutting instructions)

2½ oz. marzipan, rolled fondant, or white chocolate plastique, for the base coat (see pp. 71 and 72 for quantity)

3 oz. pale pink, pistachio, powder blue, or buttermilk rolled fondant (see p. 68), for the top coat

8 inches ivory ribbon, ⅜ inch wide

Plus:

1 recipe ivory royal icing (see pp. 76–78)

topaz luster

dipping alcohol

cocoa butter

black and white color dusts

Equipment:

small, sharp scissors

piping bag

tracing paper and fine-tip pen

pokey tool

no. 1.5 icing tip

paintbrush

Preparing the cakes

Cover each cake with a base coat of your choice, as shown on pp. 66–67, and a rolled fondant top coat (pale pink, pistachio green, powder blue, or buttermilk), as shown on p. 68. Let dry overnight. Surround each cake with ribbon, whatever the color of the rolled fondant, and fix into position with a dab of royal icing.

a

b

Decorating the cakes

1 Trace the bow template on p. 217 and use the pokey tool to mark it onto the top of each cake (a).

2 Using the pokey tool, mark around the top edge of each cake—at the corners and then two evenly spaced points along each straight side. (I found that these cakes were small enough to mark by eye rather than needing to mark them with tracing paper and a ruler.)

3 Melt the cocoa butter and color dusts together on a saucer over a saucepan of simmering water. Paint the bow on the top of each cake in white, outlining it in black (b).

4 Follow steps 2–6 on p. 137, noting that on the trinket cakes the ribbon bows and tails are added only on the corners, not at the top of each swag.

Vintage Chic

This design will really test your hand-piping royal icing skills. The cake is initially covered in royal icing to keep the edges angular, then hand decorated in a white pinstripe design before switching to a star tip for the top piped scrolls and base trail. Chic and elegant, this design transposes well to a tiered cake for a classic wedding. I have dressed this cake with a stunning handmade porcelain peony. Use silk or sugar flowers or simply lay the bridal bouquet next to the cake for maximum effect.

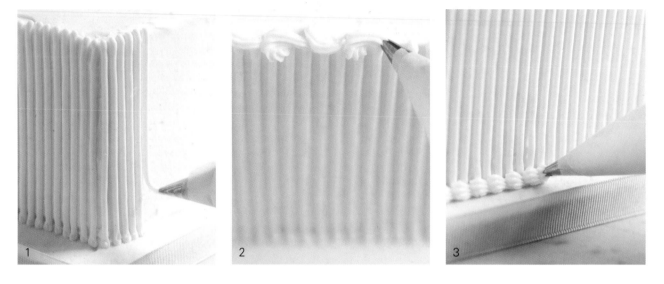

You will need:

6-inch square cake

marzipan, rolled fondant, or white chocolate plastique, for the base coat (see pp. 71 and 72 for quantity)

royal icing, for the top coat (see p. 77 for quantity)

9-inch square base board

32 inches bridal white grosgrain ribbon, ⅝ inch wide

1 recipe white royal icing (see pp. 76–77)

flower (or flowers) of your choice

Equipment:

glue stick

2 piping bags

no. 3 icing tip and no. 5 star icing tip

Preparing the cake

Place the cake in the center of the base board. Cover the cake with panels of a base coat of your choice (marzipan, rolled fondant, or chocolate plastique), as shown on p. 70. Cover the cake and board with the royal icing top coat, as shown on pp. 80–81. Surround the base board with the ribbon, fixed in place with the glue stick. Leave the cake and board to dry overnight.

Decorating the cake

1 Fit a piping bag with the no. 3 tip and fill with royal icing. Starting 1 inch from a corner, pipe the first line vertically, making contact at the top and base of the cake and allowing the line to fall and be pushed into position. (If you look closely, you will see that the piping tip and line of icing is almost at right angles to the cake, which is the perfect angle to achieve this technique). Pipe the next line parallel to the first, and continue all the way around the cake. (See p. 90 for more detailed instructions.)

2 Fit another piping bag with the no. 5 star tip and fill with more royal icing. Starting at one corner of the top, pipe alternating pressure-piped scrolls around the top edge, following the instructions on p. 92.

3 Finish by piping a uniform trail of star pearls around the base of the cake (see p. 92 for more detailed instructions). Let set overnight before dressing with a flower (or flowers) of your choice.

Georgian Lace

Architecture of the Georgian period (1714–1830) is striking for its regal symmetry. This cake has the same formal quality, combining the perfect ivory iced pearls with the repeated black flocking design of our Little Venice Cake Company lace design, and finished with a large double satin ivory ribbon and bow. Simple, striking, flawlessly decorated, and set on a black-lined board, this cake exudes class.

You will need:

4-inch, 6-inch, 8-inch, and 10-inch square cakes

4-inch, 6-inch, 8-inch, and 10-inch square cake boards

marzipan, rolled fondant, or white chocolate plastique, for the base coat (see pp. 71 and 72 for quantities)

ivory rolled fondant (see p. 68), for the top coat (see p. 72 for quantities)

14-inch square base board

black rolled fondant (see p. 68), for the base board (see p. 72 for quantity)

11 feet 6 inches black ribbon, $5/8$ inch wide

1 recipe royal icing, divided between 2 bowls and one colored ivory, the other black (see pp. 76–78)

18 doweling rods

6 feet 6 inches ivory ribbon, $1\frac{1}{2}$ inches wide

Equipment:

small, sharp scissors

glue stick

tracing paper and fine-tip pen

pokey tool

2 piping bags

nos. 1.5 and 2 icing tips

turntable

a

Preparing the cake

Place the cakes on cake boards of the same size and cover with a base coat of your choice, as shown on p. 71, and the ivory rolled fondant top coat, as shown on p. 72. Line the base board with black rolled fondant, as shown on p. 73, and edge it with 5 feet of the black ribbon, fixing it with glue. Let dry overnight.

Decorating the cake

1 Fix the base tier centrally into position on the base board with a dab of royal icing. Surround the base and the third tier with the remaining black ribbon.

2 Trace the LVCC lace design on p. 216 using the tracing paper and pen, and transfer it as a single row around the third tier and a double row around the base tier, using the pokey tool. Place the third tier on a turntable.

3 Fit a piping bag with the no. 2 icing tip and fill with black royal icing. Pressure pipe the LVCC lace design around the cake, as shown on pp. 94–95, before moving on to the base tier, piping the upper row first, then finishing with the bottom row (a). Let dry overnight.

4 Dowel and direct stack the tiers, using 6 dowels per tier, as shown on p. 83. Surround the top 2 tiers with lengths of the ivory ribbon.

5 Fit a piping bag with the no. 1.5 icing tip and fill with ivory royal icing. Start icing with the top tier. Pipe a single row of pearls around the cake directly above the ribbon and $1/8$–$1/4$ inch apart. Pipe the second row $1/8$–$1/4$ inch above the first row, spaced between the pearls of the first row. Repeat until all the sides of the cake are covered, then repeat on the second tier, keeping the rows straight and the pearls evenly spaced and sized. Let all the tiers dry overnight.

Dressing the cake

6 Make a large ribbon bow with the remaining ivory ribbon and fix into position at the base of the second tier.

Summer Butterflies

Sugar butterflies look particularly effective on individual cakes, with their wings iced into position, ready to flutter by. I have hand-painted some detail onto these butterflies and added a cluster of flowers to each cake to finish.

Preparing the cakes

Cover each cake with a base coat of your choice and the rolled fondant top coat, as shown on p. 69. Use tangerine rolled fondant for half the cakes and lime green rolled fondant for the rest. Let dry overnight.

Surround half the cakes with tangerine ribbon and the other half with lime green ribbon, and fix into position with a dab of royal icing.

Make the butterfly wings following the instructions on p. 97, making half with the orange icing and half with the green icing, but with no white markings. Let dry 4 hours.

Blend the orange and green color dusts separately with some dipping alcohol to different strengths, and brush the colors onto the butterfly wings to add shading and detail. Let dry overnight.

Decorating the cakes

1 To assemble, fit a piping bag with the no. 2 tip and fill with white royal icing. Pipe a head and body for each butterfly directly on top of a cake.

2 Gently peel the butterfly wings off the waxed paper with a small palette knife. Place one wing on either side of the body at an angle.

3 Place a small square of sponge under each wing to prop it up. Let set at least 1 hour before removing the squares.

4 Place a butterfly on each cake and fix a cluster of plunger flowers next to it with a little royal icing.

You will need (per cake):

2-inch individual round cake (see p. 69 for cutting instructions)

2½ oz. marzipan, rolled fondant, or white chocolate plastique, for the base coat

3 oz. tangerine or lime green rolled fondant (see p. 68), for the top coat

8 inches tangerine or lime green ribbon, ⅝ inch wide

Plus:

1 recipe royal icing, split into 3 bowls, and one left white, with the remaining 2 thinned to flooding consistency and colored orange and green (see pp. 76–79)

cake board

orange and green color dusts

dipping alcohol

assorted plunger flowers (see p. 105)

Equipment:

small, sharp scissors

tracing paper and fine-tip pen

masking tape

waxed paper

4 piping bags

no. 1.5 and no. 2 icing tips

paintbrush

small palette knife

sponge squares

1

2

3

Baskets in Bloom

This is the perfect cake on which to test all your newly learned skills. The tiers are covered with rolled fondant and then hand-piped with this intricate basket-weave design. The tiers are blocked with hand-molded roses studded with cut-out leaves and flooded butterflies. Impressive, gorgeous, fresh, and floral—this is perfect for any summer occasion.

You will need:

4-inch and 8-inch round cakes

4-inch and 8-inch thick round cake boards

marzipan, rolled fondant, or white chocolate plastique, for the base coat (see pp. 71 and 72 for quantities)

white rolled fondant, for the top coat and base board (see p. 72 for quantities), plus 5 oz. for a ring and a dome

12-inch round base board

39 inches green ribbon, ⅝ inch wide

3 quantities royal icing (see p. 77)

5-inch thick round cake board

6 doweling rods

25 hand-molded roses in shades of pink and lilac (see pp. 99–101), made the day before

30 cut-out rose leaves (see p. 104), made the day before

8–12 run-out butterflies (larger size) (see p. 97), made the day before

Equipment:

glue stick

4-inch and 8-inch thick round cake boards (to draw around)

pokey tool

2 piping bags

no. 3 and no. 19B (basket-weave) icing tips

paintbrush

Preparing the cake

Place the cakes on the cake boards of the same size and cover with a base coat of your choice, as shown on p. 71, and the white rolled fondant top coat, as shown on p.72. Line the base board with white rolled fondant, as shown on p. 73, and surround it with green ribbon, fixed with glue. Leave the cakes and base board to dry overnight.

Fix the base tier centrally into position on the base board using some royal icing, and fix the top tier on to the 5-inch thick round cake board in the same way. Mark around the top of both tiers by placing the spare cake boards on top of the cakes and scoring around the edge with a pokey tool.

Decorate each tier with the basket-weave design, using the piping bags and icing tips, as shown on p. 96. Let dry overnight. (Note that you will need to use more of the royal icing for fixing all the elements into position the next day.)

To assemble, dowel the base tier for stacking, and fix the top tier into position. (The deep silver board edge will still be visible at this stage.)

Decorating the cake

1 Roll 3½ oz. of the remaining white rolled fondant into a ring that will fit around the top of the base tier, ¾ inch in from the edge. Fix into position with a little water and a paintbrush (a).

2 Pipe a large pearl of royal icing onto the rolled fondant ring (b).

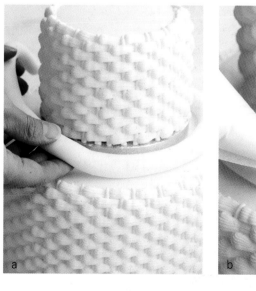

a

b

3 Fix the first rose carefully into position (c).

4 Flank this rose with several hand-cut leaves, which can either be pressed directly into the rolled fondant ring or fixed with additional royal icing to secure (d).

5 Carefully ice a flooded butterfly into position next to the flower and leaves. Continue around the cake until all the gaps are filled (e).

6 Mold the remaining 2 oz. rolled fondant into a dome and fix into position on the top tier. Add roses, leaves, and butterflies to the top to dress.

7 Fix the final butterfly, rose, and leaves to one side of the base tier.

TIP
It is worth making extra butterflies and roses, because some may well break as you are dressing the cake. Any spares can be used to dress the cake table or saved for another occasion.

Candy Cane

These hand-molded candy canes can be made well in advance of making this cake. They can also be used to decorate individual crown cakes (see p. 163), be attached to presents, or even hung on a Christmas tree. Here I have added three canes to the top of a cake, and hand-piped a loop design topped with a fleur-de-lys around the sides six times.

Preparing the cake

Place the cake on the cake board and cover with a base coat of your choice, as shown on p. 71, and the white rolled fondant top coat, as shown on p. 72. Line the base board with red rolled fondant topped with glitter, as shown on p. 73, and surround it with the ⅝-inch red ribbon, fixed with glue. Let the cake and board dry overnight.

Decorating the cake

1 To make the candy canes, knead the red and white rolled fondants separately until smooth and pliable, but not sticky. On a countertop dusted with confectioners' sugar, roll each out to a thin sausage approximately ⅛ to ¼ inch wide. Line up the red and white strands side by side and hold at both ends. Twist gently in opposite decorations to twist the strands together.

You will need:

6-inch round cake

6-inch thick round cake board

marzipan, rolled fondant, or white chocolate plastique, for the base coat (see pp. 71 and 72 for quantity)

white rolled fondant, for the top coat (see p. 72 for quantity)

9-inch round base board

red rolled fondant (see p. 68), for the base board (see p. 72 for quantity)

edible varnish

red edible glitter

32 inches red ribbon, ⅝ inch wide

2 oz. red rolled fondant

2 oz. white rolled fondant

confectioners' sugar, for dusting

royal icing, for fixing

3 red ribbon bows made with 24 inches red ribbon, ⅛ inch wide (see p. 110)

22 inches red-and-white polka dot ribbon, 1 inch wide

1 recipe red royal icing (see pp. 76–78)

Equipment:

small, sharp scissors

glue stick

ruler

sharp knife

parchment paper

2 piping bags

tracing paper and fine-tip pen

pokey tool

no. 2 icing tip

2

2 Place your hands on top and press down while rolling to seal the 2 strands of rolled fondant together, forming one smooth roll. Continue to roll the sausage until it is thinned to approximately ⅛ inch wide. You can continue to twist the roll from either end at this stage to add more twists in the pattern.

3 Cut 2½-inch lengths from the long roll and curl just the top section over to shape gently into candy canes. Let set 30 minutes on parchment paper.

4 Fill a piping bag with white royal icing, snip the end, and pipe a small pearl in the center of each candy cane. Fix the ribbon bows into position.

5 Fix the cake centrally into position on the base board and surround with the polka-dot ribbon. Trace the template on p. 218 and use the pokey tool to mark the design on the cake all the way around.

6 Fit the second piping bag with the icing tip and fill with red royal icing. Pipe the double loop of pearls shown on p. 90, and top each loop with a fleur-de-lys, piping the center pearl followed by the 2 sides. Fix the candy canes into position on the top of the cake with a dab of icing.

3

4

5

6

White and Black Berries

I particularly like the stark contrast of white and dark in this cake—making it a great design for a male celebration. Any dark fruit would work—blackberries, blueberries, or dark cherries. Choose a striking ribbon of a suitable width to bring the hand-molded white and dark collars together.

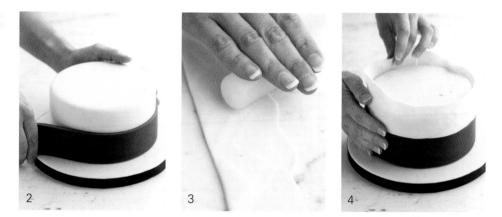

You will need:

6-inch round cake

6-inch thick round cake board

white chocolate plastique for the base coat and base board (see pp. 71 and 72 for quantities)

9-inch round base board

32 inches brown grosgrain ribbon, 5/8 inch wide

royal icing, for fixing

7 oz. dark chocolate plastique

confectioners' sugar, for dusting

brandy, for brushing

10½ oz. white chocolate plastique

22 inches decorative ribbon

14 oz. blackberries

Equipment:

small, sharp scissors

glue stick

rolling pins, large and small

sharp knife

pizza wheel

pastry brush

Preparing the cake

Place the cake on the cake board and cover with a base coat of white chocolate plastique, as shown on p. 71. Line the base board with the remaining white chocolate plastique, as shown for rolled fondant on p. 73. Surround the base board with the brown ribbon, fixed with glue. Let the cake and base board dry overnight.

Decorating the cake

1 Fix the cake centrally into position on the base board, using some royal icing. Knead the dark chocolate plastique until smooth and pliable. Shape into a long sausage on a countertop lightly dusted with confectioners' sugar, and roll out to a thickness of 1/6 inch, 24 inches long, and 2 inches wide. Trim the long edges with a pizza wheel to leave an even collar.

2 Use a pastry brush to moisten the base of the cake all the way around with brandy. Holding the dark chocolate collar in both hands, position the collar around the base of the cake, keeping it flush with the base board. Trim the collar at the back with the knife to create a clean joint.

3 Repeat step 2, using the white chocolate plastique, but this time cut only one straight edge, cutting a gentle scallop on the opposite edge instead. Switch to the smaller rolling pin and roll along the scalloped edge to thin and feather it.

4 Use a pastry brush to moisten the top half of the cake all the way around with brandy. Holding the collar in both hands, position the straight edge flush with the top of the base collar. Trim the white chocolate collar at the back with the knife to create a clean joint. Use your hands to mold the collar gently at the top of the cake to create a sense of movement.

5 Fix the length of decorative ribbon around the center of the cake to cover the joint of the collars. Fill the top of the cake with the blackberries.

White Chocolate Box

Everyone needs a showstopper in their repertoire that they can pull out of the bag for a last-minute cake. This design has to beat all others. Keep a box of chocolate cigarettes in the cupboard and use them to create an impressive cake tied with a decorative ribbon and bow and filled with fresh seasonal berries. Technically, you are not creating any of the components and the cake doesn't have to be brilliantly covered to create a glorious cake that will be admired and enjoyed.

You will need:
6-inch square cake
6-inch thick square cake board
white chocolate plastique, for the base coat (see p. 71 for quantity)
9-inch square silver base board
royal icing, for fixing
2 oz. white chocolate
80–90 (3½ oz.) white chocolate cigarettes
4 feet decorative ribbon, 1 inch wide
1¼–1½ lb fresh seasonal berries

Equipment:
pastry brush
palette knife

Preparing the cake
Place the cake on the cake board and cover with a base coat of white chocolate plastique, as shown on p. 71. Place the cake centrally on the silver base board, but do not fix in place with icing.

Decorating the cake
1 Melt the white chocolate in a bowl over a pan of gently simmering water, or in the microwave. Use a pastry brush to coat one side of the cake with melted chocolate. Position the white chocolate cigarettes perpendicular to the cake, keeping them straight and vertical. Continue to work your way around the entire cake.

2 Tie the decorative ribbon around the cake and finish with a bow. This not only adds decoration to the cake but also, and more importantly, holds the chocolate cigarettes in position while the melted white chocolate sets.

3 Fill the chocolate box with fresh seasonal berries to the desired height. Carefully lift the cake from the silver base board with a palette knife, then transfer it to a pretty glass plate.

TIPS Chocolate cigarettes usually come ready made in 4-inch lengths. Trim the cake if necessary so once covered it reaches a maximum height of 3 inches to allow the fruit to sit contained inside the cigarettes.

The cake can be prepared to the end of stage 2 up to 3 days in advance and filled with fresh berries just prior to serving.

Hedgerow

These cakes look adorable presented together on a white cake plate or glass stand. Perfect for a summer picnic, christening, baby shower, or birthday, the cakes can be boxed if not eaten on the day for each guest to take home. The molded flowers and insects can all be made well in advance—and if you are short on time, they can be used to decorate a batch of cupcakes.

You will need (per cake):

2-inch individual round cake (see p. 69 for cutting instructions)

2½ oz. marzipan, rolled fondant, or white chocolate plastique, for the base coat

3 oz. white rolled fondant, for the top coat

8-inch complementary ribbon, ⅝ inch wide

Plus:

royal icing, for fixing

bumblebees (see p. 102)

ladybugs (see p. 103)

daffodils (see p. 108)

cutter leaves (see p. 104)

poppy-style flowers (see p. 107)

buttercups (see p. 109)

plunger flowers (see p. 105)

Preparing the cakes

Cover each round cake with a base coat of your choice and the rolled fondant top coat, as shown on p. 69. Let dry overnight.

Surround each cake with ribbon and fix into position with a dab of royal icing.

Decorating the cakes

Fix the components into position on the top of each cake with royal icing.

Valentine Heart

This simple design combines hand-molded roses with hand-piped leaves to maximum effect. This cake is perfect for a romantic Valentine occasion, engagement party, or wedding anniversary. Pipe a special message inside the heart for your true love.

Preparing the cake

Place the cake on the cake board and cover with a base coat of your choice, as shown on p. 71, and the white rolled fondant top coat, as shown on p. 72. Line the base board with red rolled fondant topped with edible glitter, as shown on p. 73. Surround it with the ⅝-inch red ribbon, fixed with glue. Let the cake and board dry overnight.

Fix the cake centrally into position on the base board with some royal icing and surround the cake with the 1½-inch deep red satin ribbon. Wrap the wired ribbon around the cake and tie in a pretty bow at the front. Trim the tails with sharp scissors.

Decorating the cake

1 Trace the heart template on p. 217 and transfer onto the top of the cake using the nontoxic pencil or the pokey tool.

2 Fill a piping bag with red royal icing, snip the end off, and use to fix the red roses into position on the heart outline.

3 Fill the other piping bag with green royal icing and snip the very end as shown on p. 93 for hand piping leaves. Starting at the back of the heart, pipe small leaves around the heart of roses, as shown.

You will need:

8-inch round cake

8-inch thick round cake board

marzipan, rolled fondant, or white chocolate plastique, for the base coat (see pp. 71 and 72 for quantity)

white rolled fondant, for the top coat (see p. 72 for quantity)

12-inch round base board

red rolled fondant (see p. 68), for the base board (see p. 72 for quantity)

edible varnish

red edible glitter

39 inches red ribbon, ⅝ inch wide

1 recipe red royal icing (see pp. 76–78)

28 inches deep red satin ribbon, 1½ inches wide

5 feet red wired ribbon, 1½ inches wide

30 small hand-molded red roses (see pp. 99–101), using only one center and 2 outer petals, made the day before

1 recipe green royal icing (see pp. 76–78)

Equipment:

small, sharp scissors

glue stick

tracing paper and nontoxic pencil

pokey tool (optional)

2 piping bags

Rose Pearl Crown Cakes

Our elaborately decorated individual cakes have really taken off at Little Venice Cake Company. As a result of this, we decided that they needed a name befitting their status, rather than just "cupcakes," and have named them collectively as "crown cakes." These crown cakes are delicately hand piped with pearls and finished with hand-piped leaves and a hand-molded rose.

Preparing the cakes

Cover each round cake with a base coat of your choice and the rolled fondant top coat, as shown on p. 69. Let dry overnight.

Surround half the cakes with lilac ribbon and the other half with purple ribbon, and fix into position with a dab of royal icing. Make each hand-molded rose, which should have ⁵⁄₈-inch-diameter petals cut ¹⁄₈ inch thick, using the lilac or purple rolled fondant, as shown on pp. 99–101.

Decorating the cakes

You will need (per cake):

2-inch individual round cake (see p. 69 for cutting instructions)

2½ oz. marzipan, rolled fondant, or white chocolate plastique, for the base coat

3 oz. white rolled fondant, for the top coat

1 oz. lilac or purple rolled fondant (see p. 68), for the roses

8 inches lilac or purple ribbon, ¼ inch wide

Plus:

1 recipe white royal icing, split into 4 bowls and one colored lilac, one deep violet, one green, and one left white (see pp. 76–78)

Equipment:

small, sharp scissors

4 piping bags

3 no. 1.5 icing tips

1 Fit 3 of the piping bags with an icing tip and fill with white, lilac, and deep violet royal icing. Hand-pipe random pearls around each cake, concentrating the pearls toward the base and petering out as you near the top. Let dry 1 hour.

2 Fill the fourth piping bag with green royal icing and snip the end to create a V, as described on p. 93. Pipe 3 leaves on the top of each cake at a time.

3 Set a rose in the center of each cake on top of the leaves.

Painting the Roses Red

What a showstopper! Tiers of chocolate truffle torte are stacked together, sandwiched with lashings of chocolate ganache buttercream. The whole cake is then coated with more ganache buttercream before being wrapped in folds of finely rolled-out chocolate plastique. This outstanding creation is then dressed with delicate chocolate fans interspersed with red-glittered hand-molded chocolate roses. Inspired by *Alice in Wonderland*, this cake is certainly grand enough for the Queen of Hearts!

Preparing the cake

Line the base board with chocolate plastique and spray with edible varnish (or brush with sugar glue), then dredge with some of the red edible glitter, as shown on p. 73. Surround the board with 39 inches of the brown ribbon, fixed with glue. Let the base board dry overnight. Note that once the components are made, this cake is relatively quick to assemble, as the tiers are not precovered. For larger versions of this cake, it will be necessary to cover each tier first with chocolate plastique, then dowel and direct stack as shown on p. 83. Once stacked, it can then have an additional chocolate collar to decorate.

TIP This cake, once covered and decorated, should not be refrigerated. It should be kept at room temperature, away from direct heat sources and humidity. It will keep up to 10 days, but may begin to lose its shape over time.

You will need:

12-inch round base board

2 recipes dark chocolate plastique (see p. 75), for use as follows:
  ¼ recipe for covering the base board
  1 recipe to cover the cake
  ¾ recipe for 30 assorted chocolate fans

edible varnish or sugar glue

red edible glitter

5 feet 6 inches dark brown grosgrain ribbon, ⅝ inch wide

8-inch and two 6-inch single-depth chocolate truffle tortes (made using half the relevant quantities given in the recipe, see p. 23)

1 recipe chocolate ganache buttercream (see p. 53)

8-inch thin round cake board

confectioners' sugar or unsweetened cocoa powder, for dusting

20 red-glittered roses in assorted sizes (see pp. 99–101), made the day before

royal icing or melted chocolate, for fixing

Equipment:

small, sharp scissors

glue stick

palette knife

rolling pin

pizza wheel

small rolling pin

Decorating the cake

1 Cut one of the 6-inch cakes down to 4 inches in diameter. Trim the 3 tortes as necessary to make them level, and split in half horizontally. Spread one half of each with chocolate ganache buttercream and sandwich together. Place the base tier on the thin cake board and spread the top with more buttercream.

2 Stack the middle tier directly on top of the base tier. Spread buttercream on the top of the second tier and place the top tier into position. The middle and top tiers will not require their own cake boards, and the cake will not need to be doweled as these are only single depths and, overall, it is quite a small cake.

3 Using a palette knife, start covering the sides and visible tops of the tiers with buttercream.

4 Continue until everything is covered with a thin layer of buttercream. The finish does not need to be smooth, as all the buttercream will be covered.

5 Divide the chocolate plastique for covering the cake into 3, and knead the first part until smooth and pliable but not soft. Roll into a sausage and place on a countertop lightly dusted with confectioners' sugar or unsweetened cocoa powder. Press diagonally along the chocolate plastique in both directions with a rolling pin to flatten it slightly. This encourages the sausage to retain its shape as it is rolled. Continue to roll out the collar to a thickness of $1/8$ inch. The width should be 4 to 6 inches and the length close to 30 inches.

6 Using a pizza wheel, as this will not stretch or tear the chocolate plastique, trim one long edge so it is straight.

7 Hold the pizza wheel on the opposite long edge and draw it along in waves to create a scalloped edge.

8 Roll a small rolling pin, held just across the scalloped edge, to thin, feather, and texture the waves, pressing just lightly.

9 Lift the prepared chocolate collar carefully and wrap it around the base tier, ensuring the straight edge is flush with the base of the cake. Trim with a sharp knife so the collar joins neatly at the back of the cake.

10 Repeat, using the remaining chocolate plastique, to make 2 more collars of the same size for the remaining tiers. Fit the first one in place, working your way up the cake a little more.

11 Add the last collar, working your way up to the top and finishing with a flourish on the top tier.

12 Roll out the chocolate plastique for the fans and trim with the pizza wheel to rectangles measuring roughly 4 x 6 inches. Working quickly, so that you keep the chocolate plastique soft and pliable, fold each rectangle to make a fan and pinch the 2 shorter ends together at the base to finish.

13 Carefully place the cake in position on the base board, held in place with a dab of royal icing or melted chocolate. Surround the bottom tier with the remaining ribbon and fix with glue. Starting with the base tier, place a freshly made chocolate fan inside the collar, adhering it to the chocolate ganache buttercream on the cake.

14 Now, fix the first glitter rose in place, nestled up to the fan and facing outward. Repeat until the entire cake is dressed with fans and roses, teasing the fans into position to frame the roses, fillling the gaps, and blending all the elements well with the collar.

Chocolate Glitter Roses

Chocolate and gold have a rich affinity for premium indulgence. These crown cakes look stunning presented together at a festive party. I like to use chocolate cake, but filled with different buttercreams—vanilla, white chocolate, and coffee being my favorites.

You will need (per cake):

1½-inch individual square cake (see p. 66 for cutting instructions)

2½ oz. marzipan, rolled fondant, or white chocolate plastique, for the base coat

3 oz. dark chocolate plastique, for the top coat

8 inches dark brown grosgrain ribbon, ⅝ inch wide

12 inches gold ribbon, ⅜ inch wide

hand-molded, gold-glittered, dark chocolate roses (see pp. 99–101)

Plus:

melted dark chocolate, for fixing

Equipment:

small, sharp scissors

Preparing the cakes

Cover each cake with a base coat of your choice, as shown on pp. 66–67, and the top coat, as shown on p. 68. Let dry overnight.

Surround the cakes with the dark brown ribbon and fix in place with a dab of melted chocolate. Place the thinner gold ribbon over the brown ribbon, tie in a double knot and trim the ends with sharp scissors.

Decorating the cakes

Fix a gold-glittered dark chocolate rose into position on the top of each cake with melted dark chocolate.

Shoe Couture

A girl can never have too many shoes, so fill a shoebox with your favorite designs! We design a new collection of cakes every season for the London store Harvey Nichols. These delicate shoes are intricate and will require patience and a steady hand. Make several pairs at a time, as they do keep well.

You will need (per cake):

2-inch individual round cake (see p. 69 for cutting instructions)

2½ oz. marzipan, rolled fondant, or white chocolate plastique, for the base coat

3 oz. white rolled fondant, for the top coat

two 8 inch lengths of ribbon, chosen from a variety of widths (1 inch, ⅝ inch, ½ inch, ⅜ inch, and ¼ inch) in complementary colors

¼ oz. tan or black petal paste

Plus:

1 recipe royal icing divided between 4 bowls and colored peach, gold, black, and red (see pp. 76–78)

round glittered pearls or silver dragees

confectioners' sugar, for dusting

sugar glue

gold and purple edible glitter

Equipment:

tracing paper and fine-tip pen

piece of thin plastic or stiff cardstock

X-Acto knife

small rolling pin

2 square cake boards for drying the shoes (the size is not important as long as there is minimum 2 inch difference between the sizes)

sharp knife

5 piping bags

no. 3 and no. 1.5 icing tips

TIP If glittering any of the shoes, brush each pair with sugar glue, then dip into a bowl of glitter. Remove and shake off the excess before icing the shoes into place.

Preparing the cakes

Cover each cake with a base coat of your choice and the white rolled fondant top coat, as shown on p. 69. Let dry overnight.

Surround the cakes with double layers of ribbons, fixed in place with a dab of royal icing.

Decorating the cakes

1 Trace the shoe template on p. 218 onto a thin piece of plastic or stiff cardstock and cut out with an X-Acto knife. Knead the tan and black petal pastes until smooth and pliable, then roll them on a sugar-dusted countertop to a thickness of just ⅛ inch. Cut out 2 templates for each pair of shoes: half tan, the other half black.

2 Stack the 2 square cake boards with the smaller one centrally on top. Place the shoe soles around the edge of the cake boards as shown, shaping the soles so that the heel is on the top board and the toe on the base board. Roll a long, thin strand each of tan and black petal paste to make the heels, and cut with a sharp knife into ⅜ inch lengths. Let dry 1 hour.

3 To pipe the toes, fit 2 of the piping bags with a no. 3 tip and fill one with

peach and one with black royal icing. Using the black icing, pressure-pipe the toe of each of the black soles to fill the front of the shoe. This can then be overpiped with a bow piped from a piping bag fitted with a no. 1.5 tip and filled with red icing, decorated with a round glittered pearl (or use a silver dragee sugar decoration) or left plain. Repeat, building up the toes, using the tan royal icing on the tan soles.

4 Build up the back of each tan-soled shoe, using the remaining peach icing in a

bag fitted with a no. 1.5 tip, and the remaining black icing for each black-soled shoe, in another bag with the same-size tip. Pipe along the outline of the shoe from one side of the toe to the other, letting the icing fall into position. Pipe a second line over the first, starting and finishing a little way back. Repeat with a third and fourth line, starting each a little further back. Leave 1 hour.

5 Turn the shoes on their side and ice the heels into position. Leave 1 hour, then ice the shoes into position.

Florence Cupcake

This adorable Florence cupcake would grace any little girl's birthday party or christening. The cake features a threaded effect of ribbon and bows, with a hand-molded teddy bear holding a sugar cupcake, and sitting among more cupcakes and some pretty flowers.

You will need:

6-inch round cake

marzipan, rolled fondant, or white chocolate plastique, for the base coat (see p. 71 for quantity)

ivory rolled fondant (see p. 68), for the top coat and the base board (see p. 72 for quantities)

28 inches rose geranium ribbon, 1 inch wide

royal icing, for fixing

9-inch round base board

38 inches rose geranium ribbon, 5/8 inch wide

10 feet rose geranium ribbon, 1/8 inch wide

6 oz. petal paste, colored (see p. 68) as follows:

   2 1/4 oz. light brown

   3/4 oz. ivory

   1 1/2 oz. rose geranium pink

   1 oz. dark brown

   1/4 oz. white

   1/4 oz. black

confectioners' sugar, for dusting

strand of spaghetti

sugar glue

sugar sprinkles

6 small pink plunger flowers (see p. 105)

Equipment:

small, sharp scissors

glue stick

tracing paper and fine-tip pen

pokey tool

ribbon insertion tools

small rolling pin

3-inch frill cutter

frilling tool

1-inch round cutter

sharp knife

smiley tool

Preparing the cake

Place the cake on the cake board and cover with a base coat of your choice, as shown on p. 71, and the ivory rolled fondant top coat, as shown on p. 72. Surround the cake with the 1-inch rose geranium ribbon and fix with a dab of royal icing. Line the base board with the remaining ivory rolled fondant, as shown on p. 73, and surround with the 5/8-inch rose geranium ribbon, fixed with glue. Let the cake and board dry overnight.

Decorating the cake

Fix the cake centrally into position on the base board with royal icing. Trace the template on p. 216 and transfer onto the cake above the ribbon, using the pokey tool. Insert the 1/8-inch rose geranium ribbon, as shown on p. 111, using the ribbon insertion tools. Use the remainder of the ribbon to make 12 ribbon bows, as shown on p. 110, and use to top each ribbon loop swag.

Using the different petal pastes, make the bear components as follows:

light brown: shape into a body, head, arms, paws, ears, and muzzle; use the large and small ball tools to indent the details on the paws

ivory: shape into frosting for the 5 tiny sugar cupcakes

pink: shape into pieces for the skirt bow, and knead the rest until it is malleable, then roll out on a countertop lightly dusted with confectioners' sugar to a depth of ⅛ inch and cut out a 3-inch frill with the frill cutter

dark brown: mold some into a small triangle for the nose; reserve the rest for the cupcakes

white: shape into 2 eyes

black: shape into 2 pupils

1 Use the frilling tool positioned 1 inch within the scalloped edge to frill the edge all the way around. You may find it helpful to frill on a foam pad (see p. 107).

2 Use the round cutter in the center of the frill to remove the center.

3 Cut the frill with a sharp knife.

4 Insert a 2-inch piece of the spaghetti into the bear's body. Paint a little sugar glue around the middle of the bear's body, place the frilled skirt over the teddy bear, and press into position.

5 Position the bear's arms and paws and fix into position with sugar glue. (Note that the hind paws attach straight to the body.)

6 Spear the teddy bear's head on the spaghetti and fix with sugar glue.

7 Glue the muzzle into position, indent the smile with the smiley tool, and poke both ends of the smile with the pokey tool. Glue the nose into position.

8 Glue the ears into position and add the white and then black circles for the eyes. Fix one of the small flowers next to one of the ears.

9 Make the ribbon bow for the back of the skirt and fix into position with sugar glue.

10 To make the cupcakes, shape each base in the remaining dark brown petal paste and mark vertical lines with the pokey tool. Glue the ivory petal paste reserved for the frosting into position and brush with sugar glue. Roll the top of each cake in a small bowl of sugar sprinkles and let set. Insert a 1¼-inch length of spaghetti directly into the teddy's tummy between her arm paws, protruding outward by ⅜ inch. Slide one of the cupcakes onto the spaghetti, using sugar glue to fix.

Use the remaining sugar cupcakes and small pink flowers to dress the cake, fixing them into position with royal icing. Finally, carefully transfer the teddy bear to the cake with a palette knife and fix in place with some royal icing.

Pirate Treasure

Aye aye, Captain. This is the perfect cake for all our hero pirates, and one on which to test your hand-molding skills. Young boys will love this cake, complete with pirate, Pretty Polly parrot, treasure chest, and "X marks the spot" map.

You will need:

6-inch square cake

6-inch thick square cake board

marzipan, rolled fondant, or white chocolate plastique, for the base coat (see pp. 71 and 72 for quantity)

white rolled fondant, for the top coat (see p. 72 for quantity)

28 inches blue ribbon, 1 inch wide

1 recipe each black and gold royal icing (see pp. 76–78)

9-inch square base board

blue rolled fondant (see p. 68), for the base board (see p. 72 for quantity)

blue edible glitter

38 inches blue ribbon, ⅝ inch wide

3½ oz. gold rolled fondant (see p. 68)

1½ oz. unrefined superfine sugar

7¼ oz. petal paste, colored as follows: 2 oz. black, 1½ oz. white, 1½ oz. pale pink/peach, 1½ oz. dark brown, ¼ oz. green, ¼ oz. gold, ⅛ oz. orange and ⅛ oz. yellow

½ tsp. gold luster

1 tsp. dipping alcohol

2 inch strand of spaghetti

Equipment:

small, sharp scissors

glue stick

small rolling pin

sharp knife

sugar glue

pastry brushes

ball tool

foam pad

2 piping bags

no. 1.5 and no. 2 icing tips

pokey tool

paintbrush

smiley tool

Preparing the cake

Place the cake on the cake board and cover with a base coat of your choice, as shown on p. 71, and the white rolled fondant top coat, as shown on p. 72. Surround the cake with the 1-inch blue ribbon, fixed in place with a dab of royal icing.

Line the base board with blue rolled fondant topped with glitter, as shown on p. 73. Fix the cake centrally into position on the base board with royal icing and surround the board with the ⅝-inch blue ribbon, fixed with glue. Leave the cake and base board to dry overnight.

Decorating the cake

1 Roll out the gold rolled fondant to a thickness of ⅛ inch and trim the edges with a sharp knife to a wavy "island" shape design. Brush the top of the icing with sugar glue, using a pastry brush, and sprinkle with the sugar.

2 Brush the top of the cake with a little water, using a pastry brush, and lay the dusted rolled fondant island over the cake off center.

4

5

3 For the map, roll out a piece of the pale pink/peach paste until it is wafer thin, then frill the edges with a ball tool on a foam pad (see p. 107). Let dry 30 minutes. Fit a piping bag with the no. 1.5 tip and fill with black royal icing. Pipe the map details, then let set 1 hour.

4 Make the treasure chest using the dark brown petal paste (reserving enough for the pirate's hair) by shaping a base, approximately 1½ x 1 inch, a lid, and a roll of paste to hold the chest lid open, as shown. Roll thin strips of the gold petal paste and make 2 straps, and also a lock by pressing a pokey tool into a flattened circle of paste. Use sugar glue to fix these elements into place.

5 Fit the second piping bag with the no. 2 tip and fill with gold royal icing. Pipe small coin shapes inside the chest, and continue to build up different layers of piped coins. Let set 2 hours. Blend the gold luster and dipping alcohol together and brush over the coins, straps, and lock with a paintbrush.

3

6 To make the pirate, create the shapes as shown: body, shoulders and eye in white; legs, feet, hat, eye and eyepatch in black; head, arms, ears and nose in skin color; and curls of hair in dark brown made by rolling 5 pea-sized balls into rounded cones.

7 Fix the body into position on the legs. Use sugar glue to fix the components together. Bend the legs backward so the pirate is kneeling, and add the feet.

8 Thread the spaghetti through the body and legs to support the head. Glue the arms into position and indent the ball tool at the end.

9 Fix the head into position and use the smiley tool to add the smile.

10 Add the nose and one eye.

11 Glue the small black eye patch into position. Pinch the 4 corners of the square hat together to create a pirate hat and shape over the pirate's head.

12 Fix the pirate's hair into position, protruding from under his hat. Add the ears. Use the piping bag of black icing to pipe 2 strands to resemble the string on either side of the eye patch.

13 Assemble the parrot from its component parts of green body, wings, and tail and orange beak. Cut the piece of yellow paste into the bird's crest with a sharp knife and attach to the head. Fix the parrot into position on the pirate's shoulder and pipe 2 black eyes with the black royal icing.

14 Fix the pirate and all the other components into position on the top of the cake with royal icing.

Penguin Pudding

How cute is this Christmas cake? Our cheeky penguin, standing with his chef's hat and wooden spoon, is hand molded. The cake has been baked in a pudding mold and then covered with chocolate plastique and finished with cut-out holly leaves and glitter berries. Guaranteed to fill you with festive cheer!

You will need:

6-inch recipe of chocolate truffle torte recipe (see p. 23) cooked in a 1-pint pudding mold, 5½ inches in diameter

1 recipe dark chocolate plastique (see p. 75)

9-inch round base board

red rolled fondant (see p. 68), for the base board (see p. 72 for quantity)

edible varnish or sugar glue

red edible glitter

32 inches red ribbon, ³⁄₈ inch wide

3½ oz. white rolled fondant

confectioners' sugar, for dusting

3 oz. green rolled fondant (see p. 68)

2 oz. red rolled fondant

royal icing, for fixing

cutter white snowflakes (see p. 189), optional

For the penguin:

³⁄₄ oz. light brown petal paste

3 oz. white petal paste

3 oz. white rolled fondant

food coloring in black and orange

strand of spaghetti, broken to give a 2½-inch piece and a 1¼-inch piece

Equipment:

paintbrush (optional)

glue stick

small rolling pin

3¼-inch holly cutter

marking tool

sharp knife

pastry brush

1½-inch round cutter

Preparing the cake

Cover the cake with one coat of dark chocolate plastique, as shown on p. 71. Line the base board with red rolled fondant and top with glitter, as shown on p. 73 (reserving some for the holly berries). Surround the base board with the red ribbon, fixed with glue. Let the cake and base board dry overnight.

Knead the white rolled fondant until smooth and pliable and roll out on a countertop dusted with confectioners' sugar to approximately an 8-inch circle, ⅛ inch thick. Cut a scalloped edge all the way around. Brush the top of the cake with cooled boiled water and place the white rolled fondant into position over the top of the cake.

Decorating the cake

1 Knead the green rolled fondant until smooth and pliable and roll out to ⅛ inch thick. Cut out 3 holly leaves, using the holly leaf cutter.

1

2 Mark the indentations on the leaves with a marking tool or gently use a sharp knife . Brush the underside of the leaves with sugar glue, then fix into position on the top of the pudding as shown.

3 Roll 6 pea-sized balls of red rolled fondant and place in a small dish of the reserved red glitter to cover. Use royal icing to fix these into position on the top of the holly leaves.

4 To make the penguin, first shape the wooden spoon from the light brown petal paste, then leave it to set hard. Next, knead the white petal and white rolled fondants together thoroughly, then divide into 3 portions, weighing 3½ oz., 1½ oz. and 1 oz. Color the largest portion black and the smallest portion orange, and leave the middle one white. Now mold the different-colored pastes into the body parts, as shown: head, body, flippers, and eyes in black; beak and feet in orange; hat, eyes, and tummy (using the round cutter) in white.

5 Place the orange feet together and brush the back of them with a little sugar glue. Press the body down onto the feet to secure. Brush the body with sugar glue and fix the white tummy into position. Insert the 2½-inch length of spaghetti into the body.

6 Fix the penguin's flippers into position from the back of the body, making sure that the flippers are folded gently outward from the body.

7 Fix the head into position on top of the spaghetti. Fix the eyes and beak into position with sugar glue.

8 Insert a 1¼-inch length of spaghetti into the top of the penguin's head and fix the chef's hat into position with sugar glue. Finish by inserting the wooden spoon into the penguin's body so it sits by his flipper, as shown. Fix the cake into position offset on the base board with royal icing, and fix the penguin in position at the front. Add some white snowflakes, if using.

TIP If you don't have a holly-leaf cutter, you can cut these leaves out with a small knife freehand, or make a template from cardstock.

Crown Glitter Hearts

These cakes use the simplest technique, yet are so effective. They are guaranteed to be eye-catching, presented en masse at a birthday party or as a group of four or nine in a presentation box. Change the organza ribbon to complement the color of the party—or color-code them for boys and girls.

Preparing the cakes

Cover each cake with a base coat of your choice, as shown on pp. 66–67, and the rolled fondant top coat, as shown on pp. 68. Let dry overnight.

Surround the cakes with the organza ribbon and tie in a bow, trimming the ends neatly with the sharp scissors.

Decorating the cakes

1 Knead the gray rolled fondant until pliable but not sticky, and roll out on a clean countertop, dusted with confectioners' sugar, to a thickness of ¼ inch. Stamp heart shapes out using the cutter and place on parchment paper.

2 Spray the hearts with edible varnish or brush with sugar glue, then dredge with silver glitter. Let set before carefully removing each heart to a clean cake board to firm up, which takes 1 hour.

3 Fill a piping bag with white royal icing and snip the end. Pipe a pearl in the center of each cake and place a silver glitter heart into position.

You will need (per cake):

1½-inch individual square cake
  (see p. 66 for cutting instructions)
2½ oz. marzipan, rolled fondant,
  or white chocolate plastique, for the
  base coat
3 oz. white rolled fondant, for the
  top coat
14 inches organza ribbon, ⅝ inch wide

Plus:

1 recipe gray rolled fondant (see p. 68)
confectioners' sugar, for dusting
edible varnish or sugar glue
silver edible glitter
royal icing, for fixing

Equipment:

small, sharp scissors
rolling pin
1½-inch heart cutter
sheet of parchment paper
paintbrush (optional)
cake board
piping bag

Daffodil Easter Cake

This clever design has maximum impact for an Easter or spring celebration. I have baked the cake in a silicone Bundt mold, which creates the detailed pattern and texture on the cake. It is then frosted with lemon glacé icing and decorated with sugar daffodils, plunger flowers, and tiny ladybugs. This is a great cake to prepare ahead and make with children.

Preparing the cake
Lay a sheet of parchment paper under a wire rack, and place the cake on the rack. Spoon the glacé icing over the cake.

Decorating the cake
Place the first daffodil into position, then build up the decoration as you work around the ring, adding plunger flowers and molded ladybugs. The decorations will adhere to the icing

Let the icing set, then place the cake on a pretty plate.

You will need:

8-inch quantity of any of the cake recipes (see pp. 18–45), baked in an 8-inch silicone Bundt mold

½ recipe lemon glacé icing (see p. 58)

3 hand-molded ladybugs (see p. 103)

6 cutter daffodils (see p. 108)

plunger flowers (see p. 105) in white, yellow, and lilac, made with the following size cutters: ¼ inch, ⅓ inch, and ⅜ inch

Snowflake

This is a stylish design for a classic Christmas cake. The combination of regal purple, crisp white, and silver glitter combines well to create this striking cake. The snowflakes, which are made with cutters, trail down onto the purple-iced cake board, and the cake and board are finished with simple iced purple and white pearls.

You will need:

6-inch round cake

6-inch thick round cake board

marzipan, rolled fondant, or white chocolate plastique, for the base coat (see pp. 71 and 72 for quantity)

white rolled fondant, for the top coat (see p. 72 for quantity), plus 3 oz. for the snowflakes

3 oz. gray rolled fondant (see p. 68)

9-inch round base board

purple rolled fondant (see p. 68), for the base board (see p. 72 for quantity), plus 3 oz. for the snowflakes

32 inches purple ribbon, ⅝ inch wide

22 inches purple ribbon, 1 inch wide

1 recipe white royal icing (see p. 77)

confectioners' sugar, for dusting

edible varnish or sugar glue

silver edible glitter

white edible glitter

1 recipe purple royal icing (see pp. 77–78)

Equipment:

glue stick

small rolling pin

plunger snowflake cutters: small (¾ inch), medium (1¼ inch), and large (1¾ inch)

parchment paper

paintbrush (optional)

2 piping bags

2 no. 2 icing tips

Preparing the cake

Place the cake on the cake board and cover with a base coat of your choice, as shown on p. 71, and the white rolled fondant top coat, as shown on p. 72. Line the base board with purple rolled fondant, as shown on p. 73. Surround the base board with the ⅝-inch ribbon, fixed with glue, and surround the cake with the 1-inch ribbon, fixed with a dab of royal icing. Let the cake and base board dry overnight.

Decorating the cake

1 Fix the cake into position offset on the base board. To make the snowflakes, take the extra purple rolled fondant and knead until smooth and pliable. Roll out to a thickness of ⅛ inch on a countertop lightly dusted with confectioners' sugar. Use the plunger snowflake cutters to stamp out and indent 3 snowflakes of each size, then set aside on parchment paper dusted with confectioners' sugar to firm. Repeat with the extra white and the gray rolled fondant.

2 To glitter, place a selection of snowflakes on a sheet of parchment paper and spray with edible varnish or brush with sugar glue. Sprinkle with some of the silver or white glitter. (They don't have to be fully dredged—more just sparkling!) Glitter the white, gray, and purple snowflakes separately. Let firm about 2 hours or overnight.

3 Fit both piping bags with icing tips; fill one with white royal icing and the other with purple royal icing. Fix the snowflakes into position with corresponding colors of royal icing, starting on the top of the cake and working down over the side and onto the base board. They can overlap a bit.

4 To finish, hand pipe pearls in white and purple between and around the snowflakes, as shown on p. 90.

1

2

3

4

Crowning Glory

These simple, yet stunning, plain cakes, with their golden crowns, were part of a line we launched at Harvey Nichols. (Instructions for the candy-striped cakes and their roses, shown interspersed here, can be found on pp. 91 and 99.) You could change the mood by using the heart cutter for Valentine's Day, or perhaps bells for a wedding.

You will need (per cake):

2-inch individual round cake (see p. 69 for cutting instructions)

2½ oz. marzipan, rolled fondant, or white chocolate plastique, for the base coat

3 oz. white rolled fondant, for the top coat

8 inches red ribbon, ⅝ inch wide

8 inches blue ribbon, ⁵⁄₁₆ inch wide

¾ oz. gold rolled fondant (see p. 68)

Plus:

1 recipe gold royal icing (see pp. 77–78)

sugar glue

gold luster

dipping alcohol

Equipment:

sharp scissors

piping bag

no. 2 icing tip

1¼-inch heart cutter

sharp knife

paintbrush

Preparing the cakes

Cover each cake with a base coat of your choice and the white rolled fondant top coat, as shown on p. 69. Let dry overnight.

Decorating the cakes

1 To make each crown, roll out the gold rolled fondant to a depth of ⅛ inch, then stamp out a heart with the cutter.

2 Roll a strand of fondant to ⅛ inch thick and wind this around the top section of the crown.

3 Trim with a sharp knife and cut off the pointed base. Roll and cut a piece of fondant with tapered sides for the base of the crown. Use sugar glue to fix this into position.

4 Add another piece of fondant to build up the shape of the crown, again attaching it with sugar glue.

5 Fit the piping bag with the no. 2 tip and fill with gold royal icing. Hand pipe pearls and jewels onto the crown.

6 Pipe 2 fleurs-de-lys onto the crown, and then pipe a larger fleur-de-lys on the top (see main picture). Let dry 1 hour. Mix some gold luster and dipping alcohol on a 1:2 ratio, then brush over the decoration. Fix each crown into position on a cake with a dab of royal icing.

1

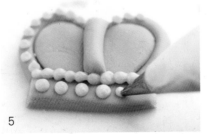
2

3

4

5

6

Frilly Citrus Roses

These tangerine and lime roses work well on plain white-iced cakes. The roses are frilled and shaped before being dusted, to create shading and texture. The centers have been made by rolling a ball of petal paste in a dish of superfine sugar mixed with color dust. Made entirely in white, these would look stunning at a summer wedding.

You will need (per cake):

2-inch individual round cake
(see p. 69 for cutting instructions)

2½ oz. marzipan, rolled fondant,
or white chocolate plastique, for the
base coat

3 oz. white rolled fondant, for the
top coat

8 inches green or orange ribbon,
⅝ inch wide

Plus:

royal icing, for fixing

orange and green petal paste, for the
roses (use the poppy method on p.
107)

2 tsp. each orange and green color dusts

dipping alcohol

sugar glue

2 tbsp. superfine sugar

Equipment:

small, sharp scissors

piping bag

paint palette

paintbrush

Preparing the cakes

Cover each cake with a base coat of your choice and the rolled fondant top coat, as shown on p. 69. Let dry overnight. Surround half the cakes with green ribbon and the other half with orange ribbon, and fix into position with a dab of royal icing.

Decorating the cakes

1 Cut out the roses from the petal paste (half in green, half in orange), and place the top layer of petals of each rose into a paint palette to dry, so that they set in a curled shape.

2 Blend together 1 teaspoon of each color dust with a little dipping alcohol (a) and brush each row of petals with color to build up the intensity (b). Fix the layers of petals together with sugar glue.

3 In a small dish, stir together half the superfine sugar with the remaining green color dust. Roll a colored ball of petal paste to the size of a small pea and brush with sugar glue before rolling it in the sugar to cover (c).

4 Fix the green petal paste ball in the center of a green rose with a dab of royal icing. Repeat to make enough green centers for half the roses, then make a similar number of orange centers.

5 Fix the flowers on top of each cake with royal icing.

Flower Power

Bright and modern, this cake combines the use of cutters with hand piping. A simple yet impactful design means that you can change the colors of the découpage flowers to complement your celebration. The tiers can be made from different recipes, with additional crown cakes made and decorated with a funky flower for guests to take home. For a more masculine version, use different-sized circles or stars, rather than flowers.

Preparing the cakes

Place the cakes on cake boards of the same size and cover with a base coat of your choice, as shown on p. 71, and the white rolled fondant top coat, as shown on p. 72. Line the base board with white rolled fondant, as shown on p. 73. Surround the base board and both tiers with the aqua ribbon, fixed with glue and royal icing respectively. Leave the cakes and base board to dry overnight.

Fix the base tier centrally into position on the base board, using some of the royal icing. To assemble, prepare the base tier for stacking, and fix the top tier into position, offset to one side (see page 82).

Decorating the cakes

1 To make the découpage flowers, knead the colored rolled fondants separately until smooth and pliable. Roll out the colors, to a depth of ⅛ inch, on a countertop dusted with confectioners' sugar. Cut out a flower with the large cutter. Then cut out a middle flower in a second color and the smallest flower in a third color. Repeat, using different combinations of sizes and colors, so you have got a good selection of flowers to work with.

2 Brush a little sugar glue onto the cake and fix the first base flower into position. Brush the center of this flower with sugar glue and fix a middle flower in place, followed by more glue and a small flower, to build up the design. Repeat randomly over the cake, using the different flowers of different sizes and colors. Work quickly to avoid the rolled fondant drying out.

3 Fit the piping bag with the icing tip and fill with the yellow royal icing. Hand pipe pearls directly on to the petals and between the flowers, to finish.

You will need:

4-inch and 8-inch round cakes

4-inch and 8-inch thick round cake boards

marzipan, rolled fondant, or white chocolate plastique, for the base coat (see pp. 71 and 72 for quantities)

white rolled fondant, for the top coat and base board (see p. 72 for quantities)

12-inch round base board

7 feet aqua ribbon, ⅝ inch wide

1 recipe yellow royal icing (see pp. 77–78)

3½ oz. each rolled fondant in aqua, orange, and yellow (see p. 68)

5-petal flower cutters: small (1 inch), medium (2 inch) and large (3 inch)

6 doweling rods

sugar glue

Equipment:

glue stick

piping bag

no. 2 icing tip

Honeybees

These hand-painted honeybee cakes were commissioned exclusively for Fortnum & Mason, as they keep hives to make their own honey on the roof of their famous building in London's Piccadilly. To show off the detail and the wings, I have chosen an aquamarine background color to cover the cakes.

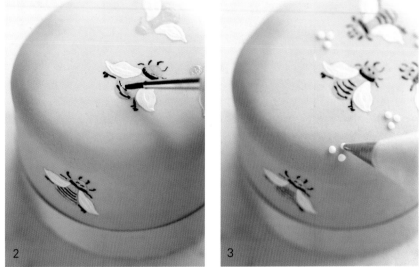

You will need (per cake):

2-inch individual round cake (see p. 69 for cutting instructions)

2½ oz. marzipan, rolled fondant, or white chocolate plastique, for the base coat

3 oz. aquamarine rolled fondant (see p. 68), for the top coat

8 inches aquamarine ribbon, 1⅝ inch wide

Plus:

1 recipe royal icing (see p. 77)

cocoa butter

white, yellow, and black color dusts

Equipment:

small, sharp scissors

tracing paper and fine-tip pen

nontoxic pencil

piping bag

no. 1.5 icing tip

medium and fine paintbrushes

Preparing the cakes

Cover each cake with a base coat of your choice and the rolled fondant top coat, as shown on p. 69. Let dry overnight. Surround each cake with ribbon and fix into position with a dab of royal icing.

Decorating the cakes

1 Trace the honeybee template on p. 212 and transfer it 4 times onto each cake—3 times clustered on the top and once on the side. Place the cocoa butter in a saucer over a pan of simmering water and add little piles of each of the color dusts around the edge.

2 Once the cocoa butter has melted, use the medium paintbrush to blend a little of it with the white color dust, then paint the honeybees' wings. Similarly, blend the other colors and paint the bodies and heads yellow (then let set 20 minutes). Finally, paint black stripes over the bodies and add the black detail with a fine paintbrush.

3 Fit the piping bag with the tip and fill with the royal icing. Hand pipe delicate white pearls between the honeybees. Let dry 1 hour.

Passion Flower

An impressive botanical cake, this design involves hand painting passion flowers and buds over two tiers. It is elegant and detailed, and so I have purposely not added any further decoration, preferring to let guests appreciate the intricacies of the painting.

Preparing the cake
Place the cake on the cake board and cover with a base coat of your choice, as shown on pp. 71, and the buttermilk rolled fondant top coat, as shown on p. 72. Line the base board with buttermilk rolled fondant, as shown on p. 73. Surround the base board and both tiers with the green ribbon, fixed with glue and a dab of royal icing respectively. Let the cakes and base board dry overnight.

Decorating the cake
1 Fix the base tier centrally into position on the base board with some royal icing. Prepare the base tier for stacking, as shown on p. 83. Trace the template on p. 215 and transfer the design onto the 2 tiers.

2 Prepare a saucer of color dusts and cocoa butter over a saucepan of simmering water, and mix the colors as required. Begin painting the base colors of the passion flowers, building up the layers.

3 Add more detail to the flowers and paint the stalks and leaves. Finish with the deeper purple strokes of the passion flower. Let set 2 hours.

4 To assemble, fix the top tier into position.

You will need:
4-inch and 8-inch round cakes

4-inch and 8-inch thick round cake boards

marzipan, rolled fondant, or white chocolate plastique, for the base coat (see p. 71 for quantities)

buttermilk rolled fondant (see p. 68), for the top coat and base board (see p. 72 for quantities)

12-inch round base board

5 feet 8 inches sage green grosgrain ribbon, 5/8 inch wide

royal icing, for fixing

6 doweling rods

color dusts in ivory, white, lilac, purple, and greens

cocoa butter

Equipment:
glue stick
assorted paintbrushes
tracing paper and fine-tip pen
nontoxic pencil

Rose Couture

This cake was inspired by an Oscar de la Renta gown with a gorgeous nipped-in waist and a full skirt adorned with bold, bright red blooms. I chose to paint the blooms on this four-tier wedding cake and blocked the base tier with open roses and ribbon loops. Changing the colors will dramatically alter this cake to personalize it for any wedding.

You will need:

4-inch, 6-inch (cut to 2 inches deep), 8-inch, and 10-inch round cakes

4-inch, 6-inch, 8-inch, and 10-inch thick round cake boards

marzipan, rolled fondant, or white chocolate plastique, for the base coat (see pp. 71 and 72 for quantity)

white rolled fondant, for the top coat and base board (see p. 72 for quantities)

8 feet 3 inches red ribbon, 5/8 inch wide

8 feet 3 inches black ribbon, 3/8 inch wide

1 quantity red royal icing (see pp. 77–78)

13-inch round base board

3 feet 8 inches black ribbon, 5/8 inch wide

18 doweling rods

6-inch round Styrofoam block, 2 inches deep

12 inches red ribbon, 1 inch wide

cocoa butter

red, black, white, and burgundy color dusts

9 oz. red rolled fondant (see p. 68)

open roses: 6 red, 6 orange, and 6 yellow (see p. 106)

triple ribbon loops with tails (see pp. 112–113), as follows:

    10 black loops using 26 feet ribbon, 3/8 inch wide

    10 red loops using 26 feet ribbon, 5/8 inch wide

    10 red organza loops using 26 feet ribbon, 1 inch wide

Equipment:

small, sharp scissors

glue stick

tracing paper and fine-tip pen

nontoxic pencil (optional)

pokey tool

4 or 5 assorted paintbrushes

piping bag

Preparing the cake

Place the cakes on the cake boards of the same size and cover with a base coat of your choice, as shown on p. 71, and the white rolled fondant top coat, as shown on p. 72. Surround all the cakes with the 5/8-inch red ribbon overlaid with the 3/8-inch black ribbon, fixed in place with a dab of royal icing. Line the base board with white rolled fondant, as shown on p. 73, and surround it with the 5/8-inch black ribbon, fixed with stick glue. Let the cakes and base board dry overnight.

Prepare the top 3 tiers for direct stacking, as shown on p. 83. Surround the Styrofoam block with the 1-inch red ribbon and fix with the glue stick. Fix the base tier centrally into position on the base board with a dab of royal icing, and prepare the base tier to be blocked, as shown on p. 82, using the Styrofoam block. Add some royal icing to the top of this block and fix the top 3 stacked tiers into position.

Decorating the cake

Trace the template of the rose on p. 214 and transfer it onto the entire cake with the pokey tool, or draw freehand with a nontoxic pencil, thinking about the layout and positioning to build up your design (see p. 115). You can always add more roses once you start painting. Prepare a saucer of color dusts and cocoa butter over a saucepan of simmering water, and mix the colors as required. Paint the design in stages, starting with the background and gradually adding depth and detail as you work, using paintbrushes of different sizes for varying effects. Remember to let the paint dry in between stages.

Dressing the cake

1 Roll 7 oz. of the red rolled fondant into a ring. Dampen the top of the base tier 3/4 inch inside the cake with a moistened paintbrush and fix the ring into position as shown.

2 Fill a piping bag with red royal icing and pipe a blob on the red rolled fondant ring. Fix the first open rose into position at an angle to bridge the gap between the third and base tiers.

4 Fix the first black ribbon loop next to the open rose by pushing it into the rolled fondant ring.

5 Add a red ribbon loop and organza ribbon loop in a similar way to fill the space, and then butt the next open rose up against the ribbons, fixed into position with royal icing.

6 Continue to work around the tier until there are no gaps.

7 Mound the remaining 2 oz. red rolled fondant into a dome for the top tier and fix into position with a little water. Push 3 red ribbon loops into a triangular position in the dome and fix 3 red open roses between the loops with royal icing. Build up the top decoration with the remaining ribbon loops. Use the sharp scissors to snip the ribbon loop tails at a nice angle to complete the decoration.

Strawberry Squares

Try these pretty hand-painted strawberry squares as an introduction to hand painting. Choose a vanilla-flavored cake filled with strawberry preserves and vanilla buttercream for the perfect summer picnic cake.

You will need (per cake):

1½-inch individual square cake (see p. 66 for cutting instructions)

2½ oz. marzipan, rolled fondant, or white chocolate plastique, for the base coat

3 oz. blue rolled fondant (see p. 68), for the top coat

8 inches green-and-white striped ribbon, ³⁄₈ inch wide

Plus:

royal icing, for fixing

red, greens, yellow, and white color dusts

cocoa butter

Equipment:

piping bag

tracing paper and fine-tip pen

nontoxic pencil

selection of paintbrushes, from medium to fine

Preparing the cakes

Cover each cake with a base coat of your choice, as shown on pp. 66–67, and the blue rolled fondant top coat, as shown on p. 68. Let dry overnight. Surround the cakes with the green and white ribbon, and fix into position with a dab of royal icing.

Decorating the cakes

1 Trace the strawberry template on p. 214 and transfer the design onto the top of each cake, using a nontoxic pencil. Be careful not to press too hard, or else the icing will crack.

2 Prepare a saucer, with the color dusts around the edge and the cocoa butter in the middle, suspended over a pan of simmering water. Mix the colors with the butter. Begin by painting the base red strawberry color onto each cake. Let dry. Add the green strawberry calyx and stalk for each cake, building up different colors of greens to create a sense of depth.

3 To finish, add the fine yellow detail to each strawberry using the finest brush.

Lovebirds

This cake gives you the opportunity to combine two techniques: a hand-painted design contained within a gilded frame, which has additional lustered hand piping. The cake would also work well with hand-painted flowers, a favorite animal or pet, or an urn of fresh, tumbling fruits.

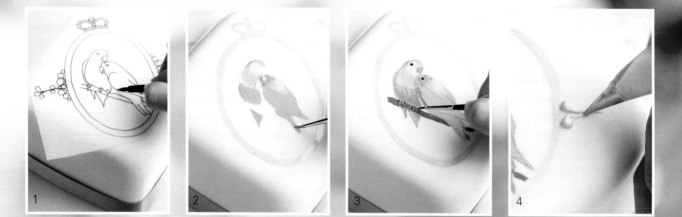

Preparing the cake
Place the cake on the cake board and cover with a base coat of your choice, as shown on p. 71, and the rolled fondant top coat, as shown on p. 72. Line the base board with white rolled fondant, as shown on p. 73. Surround the base board with the 5/8-inch gold ribbon, fixed with glue, and the cake with the 1-inch gold ribbon, fixed with a dab of royal icing. Let the cake and base board dry overnight.

Decorating the cake
1 Fix the cake centrally into position on the base board with royal icing. Trace the template on p. 212 and transfer onto the top of the cake at an angle, as shown, using a nontoxic pencil.

2 Place 1/2 teaspoon of each color dust around the edge of a saucer suspended over a saucepan of simmering water, and place the cocoa butter in the center to melt. Mix the colors for the birds, as required. Use the paintbrushes to begin painting the love birds, building up the base layers. Use the gold luster blended with cocoa butter to paint the frame and the crown.

3 Paint the final details with a very fine paintbrush, and let set.

4 Fit the piping bag with the tip and fill with gold royal icing. Pressure pipe the fleur-de-lys design on either side of the frame. Fill the rim of the frame and the crown with pearls, and also add some pearls at each corner of the cake, just above the ribbon. Let set 1 hour. Mix the gold luster and dipping alcohol together and brush the liquid over all the pearls to finish.

You will need:
6-inch square cake
6-inch thick square cake board
marzipan, rolled fondant, or white chocolate plastique, for the base coat (see pp. 71 and 72 for quantity)
white rolled fondant, for the top coat and base board (see p. 72 for quantities)
9-inch square base board
38 inches gold ribbon, 5/8 inch wide
28 inches gold ribbon, 1 inch wide
1 quantity gold royal icing (see pp. 77–78)
color dusts in yellow, pink, greens, white, blush, black, and brown
cocoa butter
1/2 tsp. gold luster
1 tsp. dipping alcohol

Equipment:
glue stick
tracing paper and fine-tip pen
nontoxic pencil
medium to fine paintbrushes
piping bag
no. 2 icing tip

True Blue

This delicate design expertly combines hand painting, hand piping, and run-outs to create a beautiful wedding cake. The top tier has painted initials surrounded with delicate butterflies, run-out flowers, and hand-piped pearls to create a découpage effect. A central column has been used to separate the top two tiers, thus elongating the cake. This design would transpose perfectly to a single-tier cake.

You will need:

4-inch, 6-inch, 8-inch, and 10-inch round cakes

4-inch, 6-inch, 8-inch, and 10-inch thick round cake boards

marzipan, rolled fondant, or white chocolate plastique, for the base coat (see pp. 71 and 72 for quantities)

ivory rolled fondant (see p. 68), for the top coat and base board (see p. 72 for quantities)

13-inch round base board

16 doweling rods

12 feet ivory ribbon, ⁵/₈ inch wide

1 recipe royal icing, divided into 2 bowls and one colored ivory and one blue (see pp. 77–78)

3-inch round Styrofoam block, 1 inch deep

5-inch round Styrofoam block, 1 inch deep

18 inches ivory ribbon, 1 inch wide

1 oz. cocoa butter

blue and white color dusts

topaz luster

dipping alcohol

Equipment:

small, sharp scissors

glue stick

3 piping bags

2 no. 1.5 icing tips

waxed paper

tracing paper and fine-tip pen

nontoxic pencil

paintbrushes

Preparing the cake

Cut the 6-inch and 10-inch cakes to a depth of 2 inches. Place all the cakes on same-size cake boards and cover with a base coat of your choice, as shown on pp. 70–71, and the ivory rolled fondant top coat, as shown on p. 72. Line the base board with ivory rolled fondant, as shown on p. 73, and edge it with ⁵/₈-inch ivory ribbon. Let the cakes and board dry overnight.

Fix the base tier centrally into position on the base board with a dab of ivory royal icing and dowel the base tier for direct stacking, using 6 of the dowels, as shown on p. 83. Surround all the tiers with ⁵/₈-inch ivory ribbon, fixed into position with a dab of royal icing. Surround both Styrofoam blocks with 1-inch wide ribbon, fixed into position with a glue stick.

Decorating the cake

1 Fit a piping bag with an icing tip and fill with some of the blue royal icing. Pipe 30 flower outlines in different sizes divided between 2 sheets of waxed paper.

2 Pipe a blue pearl in the middle of half the flowers, and set to one side.

3 Thin a little of the blue royal icing with water to flooding consistency, put it into a second piping bag and flood the remaining flowers, as shown on p. 97, using a paintbrush to ease the icing into place.

4 Fit the third piping bag with the other icing tip and fill with ivory royal icing. Pipe an ivory pearl in the center of each run-out flower. Let all the flowers dry overnight.

5

6

7

8

5 Trace the template of the butterflies and background flowers on p. 213 and transfer onto each tier with a nontoxic pencil. Melt the cocoa butter on a saucer over a pan of simmering water and blend with the blue and white color dusts around the edge of the saucer to get a range of different blues. Use the color mixtures and paintbrushes to paint in the design on the tiers.

6 Using the piping bag with the ivory royal icing, pipe additional ivory detail on the butterflies.

7 Fix the lace flowers and run-out flowers into position on each tier to build up the decoration.

8 Pipe further detail on the cake as desired. Let dry. Mix the topaz luster with enough dipping alcohol to form a runny liquid. Paint the ivory pearl detail with the topaz luster for a professional finish. To assemble, dowel the second and third tiers as shown on p. 83 for a central column, using 5 dowels for each tier. Fix the central columns into position with royal icing. Let set before stacking the tiers and presenting on a glass cake stand.

TIP
The central columns used here are the least stable of all the stacking methods, and, as such, require very careful handling. Once prepared, the cake should be assembled in its final position only for presentation. At this time, it is sensible to royal ice the tiers into position on the top of each central column. Allow time for the tier below to begin setting before proceeding with the next tier.

Templates

These templates cross-refer to the cakes in this book. Use tracing or parchment paper and a black fine-tip pen. For hand-painted designs, trace the relevant template with the pen, then turn the tracing over and place a clean sheet of paper on top so that the design shows through clearly. Trace over the back of the design with a nontoxic pencil, then trace it directly and lightly onto the surface of the cake with the pencil, leaving the impression clearly visible but avoiding denting the cake. Designs for cakes that are not hand painted should be traced with the pen and then pricked through the paper onto the cake with a pokey tool.

Honeybees p. 196

Lovebirds p. 206

True Blue p. 208

Summer Butterflies p. 144

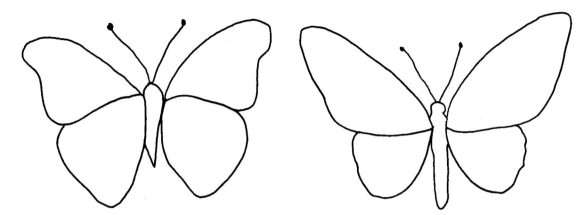

Baskets in Bloom p. 146

Strawberry Squares p. 204

Rose Couture p. 200

Passion Flower p. 198

Purple Azalea Lace p. 134
Georgian Lace p. 142

Florence Cupcake p. 172

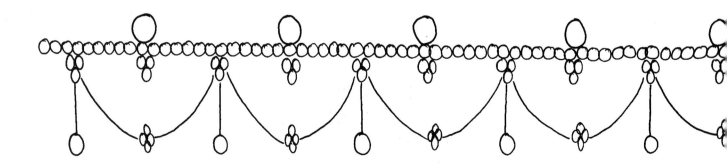

Pretty in Pink p. 124

Valentine Heart p. 160

Pompadour Trinkets p. 138

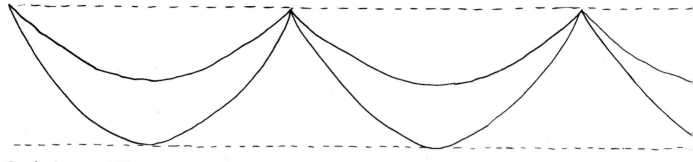

Candy Cane p. 150

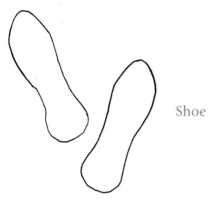

Shoe Couture p. 170

Hello, Dolly! p. 128

Art Nouveau · p. 122

Useful Addresses

A.C. MOORE ARTS & CRAFTS
Phone: 888-ACMOORE OPTION-2
www.acmoore.com
Please check Web site for store locations

BERYL'S CAKE DECORATING &
PASTRY SUPPLIES
P.O. Box 1584
North Springfield, VA 22151
Phone: 800-488-2749 /Fax: 703-750-3779
E-mail: beryls@beryls.com
www.beryls.com

BROADWAY PANHANDLER
65 East 8th Street
New York, NY 10003
Phone: 212-966-3434 / 866-COOKWARE
(266-5972)
Fax: 212-966-9017
E-mail: pisales@broadwaypanhandler.com
www.broadwaypanhandler.com

JO-ANN FABRIC AND CRAFT STORES
5555 Darrow Road
Hudson, OH 44236
Phone: 888-739-4120
Fax: 330-463-6760
www.joann.com
Please check Web site for store locations

KITCHEN KRAFTS
P.O. Box 442
Waukon, IA 52172
Phone: 800-298-5389 / 563-535-8000
Fax: 800-850-3093 / 563-535-8001
E-mail: service@kitchenkrafts.com
www.kitchenkrafts.com

MICHAELS STORES
Attn: Customer Service
8000 Bent Branch Drive
Irving, TX 75063
Phone: 800-MICHAELS (642-4235)
www.michaels.com
Please check Web site for store locations

NEW YORK CAKE AND BAKING
DISTRIBUTOR
56 West 22nd Street
New York, NY 10021
Phone: 877-NYCAKE-8/ 212-675-2253
www.nycake.com

PASTRY CHEF CENTRAL, INC.
1355 West Palmetto Park Road, Suite 302
Boca Raton, FL 33486-3303
Phone: 888-750-CHEF (2433) / 561-999-
9483
Fax: 561-999-1282
E-mail: customer_service@pastrychef.com
www.pastrychef.com

SUGARCRAFT
3665 Dixie Highway
Hamilton, OH 45015
Phone: 513-896-7089
www.sugarcraft.com

SUR LA TABLE
P.O. Box 840
Brownsburg, IN, 46112
Phone: 800-243-0852
Fax: 317-858-5521
www.surlatable.com
Please check Web site for store locations

THE ULTIMATE BAKER
4917 East 2nd Avenue
Spokane Valley, WA 99212
Phone: 866-285-COOK (2665) / 509-954-
5753
Fax: 509-532-008
www.cooksdream.com

WILLIAMS-SONOMA
Phone: 877-812-6235
Fax: 702-363-2541
www.williams-sonoma.com
Please check Web site for store locations

WILTON INDUSTRIES
2240 West 75th Street
Woodridge, IL 60517
Phone: 800-794-5866 / 630-963-1818
Fax: 888-824-9520 / 630-963-7196
E-mail: info@wilton.com
www.wilton.com

Index

Acknowledgments

My huge thanks to Jacqui Small for another stunning book! Thank you for the opportunity to publish this bible of cake decorating. Thanks to Kerenza for keeping us all on track.

Enormous thanks to the priceless Malou for your stunning photos. You, Tiggie Rose, and Kostas are well and truly part of the Little Venice family! It was a pleasure to work with you and Edyta Girgiel on this book. I shall know where to come looking for silver cake boards!

Ash–a different Everest this time–definitely summit rather than base camp! Thank you for keeping such a good eye on the crop, depth of field, and sharp focus! You have given me and my readers a very comprehensive and easy-to-follow guide to decorating.

Thank you to Allee for all the late-night edits and clear, concise instructions.

My heartfelt thanks to Lilly Swanson, Claire Murray, and Sandra Sutter, as the Little Venice Cake Company production team who worked so diligently with me to make, bake, prepare, and assist with these cakes. You are a talented, fun team and I have enjoyed every minute of working with you all.

Thank you to my Little Venice Girls, Caroline Morgan and Camilla Casey. Your constructive comments, unfaltering support, and dedication are always valued.

Thanks to my family, Phil, Marlow, and George—I love you all.

Publisher's Acknowledgments

The publisher wishes to thank Farrow & Ball and Designers Guild for the use of their beautiful wallpapers.

Picture Credits

All photography by Malou Burger, excluding the following images, by Polly Wreford: Pages 2, 87 top left and bottom left, 106, 112–117, 119 top center, bottom left, and bottom right, 122–123, 128, 130 bottom, 131, 134, 135 left, 162, 200–203.